The

Long

Poem

Anthology

The
Long
Poem
Anthology
edited
by
Michael
Ondaatje

The Coach House Press   Toronto

Grateful acknowledgement is made for permission to reprint,
to Turnstone Press, for *Seed Catalogue* (1977) by Robert Kroetsch;
to Talon Books, for *Steveston* (1974) by Daphne Marlatt;
to Applegarth Press, for *Long Sault* (1975) by Don McKay;
to Open Space, for *The Moth Poem* (1964) by Robin Blaser;
and to Talon Books, for *King of Swords* (1972) by Frank Davey.
   The Intervals by Stuart MacKinnon, *The Fontainebleau Dream
Machine* by Roy Kiyooka and *The Martyrology Book IV* by bpNichol
were originally published by The Coach House Press.

Published with the assistance of the Canada Council
and the Ontario Arts Council.

ISBN 0-88910-177-9

Sennett took me aside and explained their method of working. 'We have no scenario – we get an idea then follow the natural sequence of events until it leads up to a chase, which is the essence of our comedy.'

This method was edifying, but personally I hated a chase. It dissipates one's personality; little as I knew about movies, I knew that nothing transcended personality.

CHARLIE CHAPLIN

Contents

Michael Ondaatje: Introduction   9

Robert Kroetsch: Seed Catalogue   19

Stuart MacKinnon: The Intervals   45

Daphne Marlatt: Steveston   81

Don McKay: Long Sault   125

Robin Blaser: The Moth Poem   159

Frank Davey: King of Swords   181

George Bowering: Allophanes   203

Roy Kiyooka: The Fontainebleau Dream Machine   245

bpNichol: The Martyrology Book iv   267

Statements by the Poets   309

Recommended Reading   341

Michael Ondaatje
Introduction

What is in the Pot

'In planning a book — or an escape —', says Calvino's Count of
Monte Cristo, ' — the first thing to know is what to exclude'.
Exclusion was not just the first problem in putting this book
together. Long poems crawl out of cupboards, archives, gardens, long bus journeys, out of every segment of Canadian
writing. And yet it is a form or a 'size' or 'structure' that has
been politely ignored by anthologists, schools, and the general
reading public. This wouldn't matter if not much was happening with the form, but it seems to me that the most interesting
writing being done by poets today can be found within the
structure of the long poem. Canada supposedly sparked the
idea for Imagism but it is really not the country for the haiku.
After the perfect lines about the frog or cricket or eclipse we
turn around and have to come to terms with the vastness of our
place or our vast unspoken history.

Our best poetry, after we stopped being cocky with narrative,
is involved with process and perspective. Reaney gave us a
Shepherd's Calendar, Webb gave us Naked Poems, Gottlieb a
collage of street songs, Livesay a moral history of the 30's and
40's, and Lionel Kearns gave us a friend whispering 'Listen
George'. Birney moved from 'David' to 'November Walk Near
False Creek Mouth'. These writers mapped out possible directions that became important to a new generation of poets.
They were important because they were personal, transitional,
and local. They went their own way sliding along on the character of the speaker; they were poems (in Bowering's phrase)
which did not seem 'to be peering thru a crenel at the passing
show'.

There are numerous ways to select poems for an anthology.
One approach might have been chronological or historical. In
the end, though, I decided to be governed by curiosity. Any long
project for me has to be generated by a sense of discovery, of
learning about something I'm not sure of, don't fully understand. The same motive lies behind this book. I wanted to
explore the poets who surprise me with their step, their process. That is what draws these nine together. These poems

are not parading down the main street. Some jeer anonymously from the stands, some are written in such frail faint pencil that one can barely hold them, they shift like mercury off the hand. The stories within the poems don't matter, the grand themes don't matter. The movement of the mind and language is what is important – as in a McFadden poem or Birney's 'November Walk ...' We can come back to these fragile drawings again and again, taking another look, discovering something new, not hearing what we heard the first time we read it. Somehow the poems move when you are not watching so that new objects and tones come into relief. We are not dealing with poetry whose themes are hardened into stone, into a public cultural voice. Between readings the tents are folded and the company moves on. In the daylight sometimes one can hardly see them at all.

Something did happen in the 70's that has gone unrecognised by most academic readers of poetry. Some writers became public personalities; but at the same time some poets – from the generation of Souster's *New Wave Canada* – turned inward, away from the individual occasional poem, to explore, to take a longer look at themselves and their landscape, to hold onto something frail – whether the memory or discovery of a place, or a way of speaking. They emerged with these works and published them – mostly with small presses across the country.

These private explorations are among the most significant poetry of recent years, and this book represents some of those 'unofficial' voices of the 70's. (The exception is Blaser's *The Moth Poem* which was published in 1964. I would also have liked to have included Phyllis Webb's *Naked Poems* 1965 but was unable to; to me it is still one of the most beautiful and influential books of the last decade). These nine poems were not of course the only ones – there were numerous poem sequences, prose sequences, and other long poems that could have been included: Lee's elegy to Ladoo, Thompson's ghazals posthumously published as *StiltJack,* work by McFadden, Atwood, Geddes, Helwig, Barry McKinnon, Brian Fawcett, Gerry Gilbert, Fred Wah, Lionel Kearns, Christopher Dewdney, Andy Suknaski ...

2

I people
this room
with things, a
chair, a lamp, a
fly   two books by
Marianne Moore.
PHYLLIS WEBB, *Naked Poems* (1965)

Most of the poets have few dramatic props. Kiyooka says his
work is 'a musical score for a small ensemble. a window, sky-
light and an open door.' But while the landscape may be small
and specific, everything can enter the poem – whether it is the
range of history in Davey or the vistas of Kiyooka's dream
journey. 'All of the poem's elements', writes Davey, 'are happening on the day of the poem's writing.' In Nichol's recent *Book
of Hours* he selects a precise time or space but allows anything
to fly in, he makes room for numerous entrances and exits.
(In one of the poems he quotes a line from a science-fiction
novel which speaks of the need to whip 'order' into a yelping
pack of probabilities.)

Margaret Avison has said that literature results when 'every
word is written in the full light of *all* a writer knows.' These
poems show a process of knowledge, of discovery during the
actual writing of the poem. 'You have to go into a serial poem
not knowing what the hell you're doing', wrote Jack Spicer. The
poets do not fully know what they are trying to hold until they
near the end of the poem, and this uncertainty, this lack of
professional intent, is what allows them to go deep. The poems
have more to do with open fields and quiet rooms than public
stages. In the 70's some poets talked out loud and some listened. These poets listen to everything. Kroetsch hangs around
bars picking up stories like Polonius behind the curtain, others
recall childhood language, or hold onto dreams after they have
awakened, or speak the unsaid politics of the day. They tempt
quiet things out of the corner. 'It is not easy to catch dogs when
it is your business to catch dogs', said Steinbeck.

3

According to Jack, 'You have to go into a serial poem not knowing what the hell you're doing.' 'You have to be tricked into it, it has to be some path that you've never seen on a map before ...' It has to be a renewed language and information that becomes a kind of map. Ideally Jack worked in that long form without looking back and without thought of the previous poem, so that the poet could be led by what was composing. The serial poem is often like a series of rooms where the lights go on and off. It is also a sequence of energies which burn out, and it may, by the path it takes, include the constellated. There is further a special analogy with serial music: the voice or tongue, the tone, of the poem sounds individually, as alone and small as the poet is .. but sounded in series, it enters a field ... A 'necessary world' is composed in the serial poem.

ROBIN BLASER, 'The Practice of Outside'
in *The Collected Books of Jack Spicer*

The trick naturally is what Duncan learned years ago and tried to teach us – not to search for the perfect poem but to let your way of writing of the moment go along its own paths, explore and retreat but never be fully realized (confined) within the boundaries of one poem ... There is really no single poem.

That is why all my stuff from the past (except the *Elegies* and *Troilus*) looks foul to me. The poems belong nowhere. They are one-night stands filled (the best of them) with their own emotions, but pointing nowhere, as meaningless as sex in a Turkish bath. It was not my anger or my frustration that got in the way of my poetry but the fact that I viewed each anger and each frustration as unique – something to be converted into poetry as one would exchange foreign money. I learned this from the English Department (and from the English Department of the spirit – that great quagmire that lurks at the bottom of all of us) and it ruined ten years of my poetry. Look at those other poems. Admire them if you like. They are beautiful but dumb.

Poems should echo and re-echo against each other. They should create resonances. They cannot live alone any more than we can ....

Things fit together. We knew that – it is the principle of magic.
Two inconsequential things can combine together to become a consequence. This is true of poems too. A poem is never to be judged by
itself alone. A poem is never by itself alone.
JACK SPICER, *Admonitions*

4

In a country with an absurd history of film, real film goes
underground. And it comes up often in strange clothes – sometimes as theatre, sometimes as poetry. Theatre companies
such as Passe Muraille, writers such as Marlatt and Kroetsch
and McKay, are our true documenters. Michel Brault's *Les
Ordres* has more in common with the politics of MacKinnon's
The Intervals than most 'official' films of English Canada.
Dorothy Livesay in her article on the documentary poem in
Canada has already spoken of this tradition and her own poems
such as 'Call My People Home' are early examples of the form.
What is needed now is perhaps a new look at the documentary
poem in Canada – how it has changed in intent, how it has
become (in Susan Sontag's term) 'infradidactic'. For in spite of
the poems being *long,* there is little evidence of a didactic
formal voice. Personalities are charted by naming objects.
That is, if you speak of a couple who have a John Boyle postcard
taped to the fridge you are saying more about the couple and
what they probably think than what might be said in five
paragraphs on their political thought. In Nichol's introduction
to the *Martyrology* Book III he gives us that lovely list, the easy
times suggested in the spaces between the lines, in the pleasure of the naming:

carrots onions celery potatoes
cheddar cheese
beef for stock
salt pepper garlic

windy day
keep the door open
kitchen cool

core & steam the vegetables
peel the leaves
rice & vegetables for the hollopchis

sit around the table
talk of nothing
good feeling for the job that's done

walk the fields the wind blows
blue sky above you always
pray that will be so

These poems expect you to fill in the silences. In some cases
you are offered the clothes (a place or a dream), and you must
step forward and dress yourself. Perhaps the documentary will
always be a new form and perhaps (along with the lyric) it will
always have to be one step ahead of the 'black steel lines of
fiction.' Documentaries probe and explore and argue their way
through a contemporary situation. Livesay argued with her
world, Fawcett argues with his. Things haven't changed. The
documentary, as the filmmaker Godard says, is 'a road leading
to fiction, but it's still not a road, it's bushes and trees.' The need
to chart what is around us, to say what is in the pot, creates at
first strange bedfellows with the contemporary poetic voice.
However one should remember that Nichol, who has spent
years landscaping *The Martyrology,* used to be a cross-country
runner. Or that George Bowering was an aerial photographer
for the air force. Kroetsch dutifully planted bulbs and waited
patiently for spring. McKay on the other hand saw his landscape erased, not created. The physical world, its habit, what is
'given', is the map or backdrop to these poems. If you forget
that, you may assume that these poets are just pissing on the
Porsche of Canadian literature.

5

Ever since I read it a year ago I've been thinking of a paragraph Jean McKay wrote in a review in *Brick* magazine. It is a beautiful statement on the problem of the contemporary writer-reader in his relationship to the more relaxed writing of his childhood.

... it makes me sad. The old gentle story-telling is disappearing. It's partly because it's outmoded as a literary style. But also to view life in all its complexity with equanimity takes I think a lot more strength nowadays than it used to. I grew up on Walt Kelly, along with O. Henry and Thurber and Twain and Leacock: writers who were absorbed with the passing human scene, but who knew how to *take it easy*. Like Faulkner's Ratcliff, peddling sewing machines up and down the country, watching shrewdly as he went, collecting and sorting; shaping the ironies of people's lives into stories, and telling them, telling them slow enough to be accurate, slow enough to enjoy the telling.

In some way the old gentle story, 'slow enough to enjoy the telling' has an affinity with the long poem. Although the footwork may be faster or now include the absurd connections seen every day in the real world, the business of 'collecting' and 'sorting' applies *here* more than in most of the poems of our time. What Jean McKay desires in that paragraph is strangely not too far from Robin Blaser's remark that 'suddenly, in the contemporary experience, the formal, public language does not hold and our language in the midst of a recomposition has to account for what is stopped, lost, loose and silent.' These poets – contemporary and experimental – in some way bring their experiments *home*, establishing in pencil a new bedrock of beliefs.

There is a novel by the radical German dramatist Peter Handke called *Short Letter, Long Farewell*. In it a young German travels through America. Everything is displaced and he and his companions record it – with Polaroid snaps, stark meaningless images, with paranoia. In the end, after this mad journey, he and his estranged wife go to vist the great classic film director John Ford. They tell Ford of their experiences. 'Ah Gott' says Ford – and we are not sure if he is shocked, or objects to being introduced to a totally alien world, or has learned something. The point is Handke is not just saying that Ford can teach us something with his classicism. He wants to teach Ford something. He hopes that Ford realises he could learn something from Handke.

MICHAEL ONDAATJE, 1979

Robert Kroetsch
Seed Catalogue

1

No. 176 *Copenhagen Market Cabbage:* This
new introduction, strictly speaking, is in every
respect a *thoroughbred,* a *cabbage* of *highest
pedigree,* and is *creating considerable flurry*
among *professional gardeners* all *over the
world.*

We took the storm windows/off
the south side of the house
and put them on the hotbed.
Then it was spring. Or, no:
then winter was ending.

     'I wish to say we had lovely success
     this summer with the seed purchased
     of you. We had the finest Sweet
     Corn in the country, and Cabbage
     were dandy.'
     — W.W. Lyon, South Junction, Man.

     My mother said:
     Did you wash your ears?
     You could grow cabbages
     in those ears.

Winter was ending.
This is what happened:
we were harrowing the garden.
You've got to understand this:
I was sitting on the horse.
The horse was standing still.
I fell off.

     The hired man laughed: how
     in hell did you manage to
     fall off a horse that was
     standing still?

Bring me the radish seeds,
my mother whispered.

Into the dark of January
the seed catalogue bloomed

a winter proposition, if
spring should come, then,

with illustrations:

No. 25 *McKenzie's Improved Golden Wax Bean:*
THE MOST PRIZED OF ALL BEANS. *Virtue* is its
own reward. We have had *many expressions*
from *keen discriminating gardeners extolling*
our seed and *this variety.*

Beans, beans,
the musical fruit;
the more you eat,
the more you virtue.

My mother was marking the first row
with a piece of binder twine, stretched
between two pegs.

The hired man laughed: just
about planted the little bugger.
Cover him up and see what grows.

My father didn't laugh. He was puzzled
by any garden that was smaller than a
quarter section of wheat and summerfallow.

the home place: N.E. 17-42-16-w4th Meridian.

the home place: one and a half miles west of Heisler, Alberta,
on the correction line road
and three miles south.

No trees
around the house.
Only the wind.
Only the January snow.
Only the summer sun.
The home place:
a terrible symmetry.

How do you grow a gardener?

        Telephone Peas
        Garden Gem Carrots
        Early Snowcap Cauliflower
        Perfection Globe Onions
        Hubbard Squash
        Early Ohio Potatoes

This is what happened – at my mother's wake. This
is a fact – the World Series was in progress. The
Cincinnati Reds were playing the Detroit Tigers.
It was raining. The road to the graveyard was barely
passable. The horse was standing still. Bring me
the radish seeds, my mother whispered.

2

My father was mad at the badger: the badger was digging holes in the potato patch, threatening man and beast with broken limbs (I quote). My father took the double-barrelled shotgun out into the potato patch and waited.

Every time the badger stood up, it looked like a little man, come out of the ground. Why, my father asked himself – Why would so fine a fellow live under the ground? Just for the cool of roots? The solace of dark tunnels? The blood of gophers?

My father couldn't shoot the badger. He uncocked the shotgun, came back to the house in time for breakfast. The badger dug another hole. My father got mad again. They carried on like that all summer.

> *Love is an amplification*
> *by doing/ over and over.*
>
> *Love is a standing up*
> *to the loaded gun.*
>
> *Love is a burrowing.*

One morning my father actually shot at the badger. He killed a magpie that was pecking away at a horse turd about fifty feet beyond and to the right of the spot where the badger had been standing.

A week later my father told the story again. In that version he intended to hit the magpie. Magpies, he explained, are a nuisance. They eat robins' eggs. They're harder to kill than snakes, jumping around the way they do, nothing but feathers.

Just call me sure-shot, my father added.

3

No. 1248 *Hubbard Squash:* As *mankind* seems
to have a *particular fondness* for squash, *Nature*
appears to have *especially* provided this *match-
less* variety of *superlative flavor.*

> *Love is a leaping up*
> *and down.*
>
> *Love*
> *is a beak in the warm flesh.*

As a cooker, it heads the list for warted squash.
The vines are of strong running growth; the
fruits are large, olive shaped, of a deep rich green
color, the rind is smooth ...

But how do you grow a lover?

This is the God's own truth:
playing dirty is a mortal sin
the priest told us, you'll go to hell
and burn forever (with illustrations) —

it was our second day of catechism
— Germaine and I went home that
afternoon   if it's that bad, we
said to each other   we realized
we better quit   we realized

let's do it just one last time
and quit.

This is the God's own truth:
catechism, they called it,
the boys had to sit in the pews
on the right, the girls on the left.
Souls were like underwear that you
wore inside. If boys and girls sat
together —

Adam and Eve got caught
playing dirty.

This is the truth.
We climbed up into a granary
full of wheat   to the gunny sacks
the binder twine was shipped in –

we spread the paper from the sacks
smooth sheets   on the soft wheat
Germaine and I   we were like/one

we had discovered, don't ask me
how, where – but when the priest said
playing dirty we knew – well –

he had named it   he had named
our world   out of existence
(the horse   was standing still)

– This is my first confession. Bless me father I played
  dirty so long, just the other day, up in the granary
  there by the car shed – up there on the Brantford Binder
  Twine gunny sacks and the sheets of paper – Germaine
  with her dress up and her bloomers down –

– Son. For penance, keep your peter in your pants
  for the next thirteen years.

But how –

> Adam and Eve and Pinch-Me
> went down to the river to swim –
> Adam and Eve got drownded.

But how do you grow a lover?

> We decided we could do it
> just one last time.

4

It arrived in winter, the seed catalogue, on a January
day. It came into town on the afternoon train.

Mary Hauck, when she came west from Bruce County, Ontario,
arrived in town on a January day. She brought along
her hope chest.

She was cooking in the Heisler Hotel. The Heisler Hotel
burned down on the night of June 21, 1919. Everything
in between: lost. Everything: an absence

of satin sheets
of embroidered pillow cases
of tea towels and English china
of silver serving spoons.

How do you grow a prairie town?

        The gopher was the model.
        Stand up straight:
        telephone poles
        grain elevators
        church steeples.
        Vanish, suddenly: the
        gopher was the model.

How do you grow a past/
to live in

the absence of silkworms
the absence of clay and wattles (whatever the hell
            they are)
the absence of Lord Nelson
the absence of kings and queens
the absence of a bottle opener, and me with a vicious
            attack of the 26-ounce flu
the absence of both Sartre and Heidegger
the absence of pyramids
the absence of lions
the absence of lutes, violas and xylophones
the absence of a condom dispenser in the Lethbridge Hotel
            and me about to screw an old Blood whore.
            I was in love.
the absence of the Parthenon, not to mention the Cathé-
            drale de Chartres
the absence of psychiatrists
the absence of sailing ships
the absence of books, journals, daily newspapers and every-
            thing else but the *Free Press Prairie Farmer*
            and *The Western Producer*
the absence of gallows (with apologies to Louis Riel)
the absence of goldsmiths
the absence of the girl who said that if the Edmonton
            Eskimos won the Grey Cup she'd let me kiss
            her nipples in the foyer of the Palliser
            Hotel. I don't know where she got to.
the absence of Heraclitus
the absence of the Seine, the Rhine, the Danube, the Tiber
            and the Thames. Shit, the Battle River ran
            dry one fall. The Strauss boy could piss
            across it. He could piss higher on a barn
            wall than any of us. He could piss right
            clean over the principal's new car.
the absence of ballet and opera
the absence of Aeneas

How do you grow a prairie town?

Rebuild the hotel when it burns down. Bigger. Fill it
full of a lot of A-1 Hard Northern Bullshitters.

— You ever hear the one about the woman who buried
her husband with his ass sticking out of the ground
so that every time she happened to walk by she could
give it a swift kick?

— Yeh, I heard it.

5

I planted some melons, just to see what would
happen. Gophers ate everything.

> I applied to the Government.
> I wanted to become a postman,
> to deliver real words
> to real people.

> There was no one to receive
> my application.

I don't give a damn if I do die do die do die do die do die
do die do die do die do die do die do die do die do die do
die do die do die do die do die do die do die do die do die
do

6

No. 339 *McKenzie's Pedigreed Early Snowcap
Cauliflower:* Of the many *varieties* of *vegetables* in *existence, Cauliflower* is *unquestion-
ably* one of the *greatest inheritances* of the *present generation, particularly Western Canadians.*
There is *no place* in the *world* where *better
cauliflowers* can be *grown* than right here in the
West. The *finest specimens* we have *ever seen,*
larger and of *better quality,* are *annually grown*
here on our *prairies.* Being *particularly* a *high
altitude plant* it *thrives* to a *point* of *perfection*
here, *seldom seen* in *warmer climes.*

But how do you grow a poet?

Start: with an invocation
invoke –

His muse is
his muse/if
memory is

and you have
no memory then
no meditation
no song (shit
we're up against it)

                    how about that girl
                    you felt up in the
                    school barn or that
                    girl you necked with
                    out by Hastings' slough
                    and ran out of gas with
                    and nearly froze to
                    death with/ or that
                    girl in the skating
                    rink shack who had on
                    so much underwear you
                    didn't have enough
                    prick to get past her/
                    CCM skates

Once upon a time in the village of Heisler –

– Hey, wait a minute.
That's a story.

How do you grow a poet?

> For appetite: cod-liver
> oil.
> For bronchitis: mustard
> plasters.
> For pallor and failure to fill
> the woodbox: sulphur & molasses.
> For self-abuse: ten Our Fathers &
> ten Hail Marys.
> For regular bowels: Sunny Boy
> Cereal.

How do you grow a poet?

'It's a pleasure to advise that I
won the First Prize at the Calgary
Horticultural Show ... This is my
first attempt. I used your seeds.'

> Son, this is a crowbar.
> This is a willow fencepost.
> This is a sledge.
> This is a roll of barbed wire.
> This is a bag of staples.
> This is a claw hammer.

We give form to this land by running
a series of posts and three strands
of barbed wire around a quarter-section.

> First off I want you to take that
> crowbar and drive 1,156 holes
> in that gumbo.
> And the next time you want to
> write a poem
> we'll start the haying.

How do you grow a poet?

> This is a prairie road.
> This road is the shortest distance
> between nowhere and nowhere.
> This road is a poem.
>
> Just two miles up the road
> you'll find a porcupine
> dead in the ditch. It was
> trying to cross the road.

As for the poet himself
we can find no record
of his having traversed
the land/in either direction

no trace of his coming
or going/only a scarred
page, a spoor of wording
a reduction to mere black

and white/a pile of rabbit
turds that tells us
all spring long
where the track was

poet ... say uncle.

How?

Rudy Wiebe: 'You must lay great black steel lines of
fiction, break up that space with huge design and, like
the fiction of the Russian steppes, build a giant
artifact. No song can do that ..'

February 14, 1976. Rudy, you
took us there: to the Oldman River
Lorna & Byrna, Ralph & Steve and me
you showed us where
the Bloods surprised the Crees
in the next coulee/surprised
them to death. And after
you showed us Rilke's word
Lebensgliedes.

Rudy: Nature thou art.

7

Brome Grass (Bromus Inermis): No amount of
cold will kill it. It *withstands* the summer suns.
Water may stand on it for several weeks without
apparent injury. The roots push through the soil,
throwing up new plants continually. It *starts
quicker* than other grasses in the spring. *Remains green* longer in the fall. *Flourishes under
absolute neglect.*

The end of winter:
seeding/time.

*How do you grow
a poet?*

(a)

I was drinking with Al Purdy. We went round and round
in the restaurant on top of the Chateau Lacombe. We
were the turning center in the still world, the winter
of Edmonton was hardly enough to cool our out-sights.

The waitress asked us to leave. She was rather insistent;
we were bad for business, shouting poems at the paying
customers. Twice, Purdy galloped a Cariboo horse
right straight through the dining area.

Now that's what I call
a piss-up.

'No song can do that.'

(b)

No. 2362 *Imperialis Morning Glory:* This is the
wonderful *Japanese Morning Glory,* celebrated
the world over for its *wondrous beauty* of both
flowers and foliage.

Sunday, January 12, 1975. This evening after
rereading *The Double Hook*: looking at Japanese prints.
Not at actors. Not at courtesans. Rather: Hiroshige's
series, *Fifty-Three Stations on the Tokaido.*

From the *Tokaido* series: 'Shono-Haku-u.' The
bare-assed travellers, caught in a sudden shower.
Men and trees, bending. How it is in a rain shower/
that you didn't see coming. And couldn't have avoided/
even if you had.

   The double hook:
   the home place.

   The stations of the way:
   the other garden

   Flourishes.
   Under absolute neglect.

(c)

Jim Bacque said (I was waiting for a plane,
after a reading; Terminal 2, Toronto) — he said,
You've got to deliver the pain to some woman,
don't you?

— Hey, Lady.
  You at the end of the bar.
  I wanna tell you something.

— Yuh?

— Pete Knight — of Crossfield,
  Alberta. Bronc-Busting Champion
  of the World. You ever hear of
  Pete Knight, the King of All
  Cowboys, Bronc-Busting Champion
  of the World?

— Huh-uh.

— You know what I mean? King
  of *All* Cowboys ... Got
  killed — by a horse.
  He fell off.

— You some kind of nut
  or something?

8

> We silence words
> by writing them down.

THIS IS THE LAST WILL AND TESTAMENT
OF ME, HENRY L. KROETSCH:

(a) [yes, his first bequest]

To my son Frederick my carpenter tools.

It was his first bequest. First,
a man must build.

Those horse-barns around Heisler –
those perfectly designed barns
with the rounded roofs – only Freddie
knew how to build them. He mapped
the parklands with perfect horse-barns.

> I remember my Uncle Freddie.
> (The farmers no longer
> use horses.)

> Back in the 30s, I remember
> he didn't have enough money
> to buy a pound of coffee.

> Every morning at breakfast
> he drank a cup of hot water
> with cream and sugar in it.

> Why, I asked him one morning –
> I wasn't all that old – why
> do you do that? I asked him.

> Jesus Christ, he said. He was
> a gentle man, really. Don't you
> understand *anything*?

9

The danger of merely living.

a shell/exploding
in the black sky: a
strange planting

a bomb/exploding
in the earth: a
strange

man/falling
on the city.
Killed him dead.

It was a strange
planting.

the absence of my cousin who was shot down while bombing
the city that was his maternal great-grandmother's
birthplace. He was the navigator. He guided himself
to that fatal occasion:
                    — a city he had
                      forgotten
                    — a woman he had
                      forgotten

He intended merely to release a cargo of bombs on a
target and depart. The exploding shell was:

a) an intrusion on a design that was not his, or

b) an occurrence which he had in fact, unintentionally,
   himself designed, or

c) it is essential that we understand this matter
   because:

He was the first descendant of that family to return
to the Old Country. He took with him: a cargo of bombs.

Anna Weller: *Geboren* Cologne, 1849.
Kenneth MacDonald: Died Cologne, 1943.

A terrible symmetry.

A strange muse: forgetfulness. Feeding her far children
to ancestral guns, blasting them out of the sky, smack/
into the earth. Oh, she was the mothering sort. Blood/
on her green thumb.

10

After the bomb/blossoms *Poet, teach us*
After the city/falls   *to love our dying.*
After the rider/falls
(the horse   *West is a winter place.*
standing still)   *The palimpsest of prairie*

                       under the quick erasure
                       of snow, invites a flight.

How/do you grow a garden?

(a)

No. 3060 *Spencer Sweet Pea:* Pkt. $.10; oz. $.25;
quarter lb. $.75; half lb. $1.25.

Your sweet peas
climbing the staked
chicken wire,
climbing the stretched
binder twine by
the front porch

taught me the smell
of morning, the grace
of your tired
hands, the strength
of a noon sun, the
color of prairie grass

taught me the smell
of my sweating armpits.

(b)

How do you a garden grow?
How do you grow a garden?

'Dear Sir,
   The longest brome grass I remember seeing was
one night in Brooks. We were on our way up to the Calgary
Stampede, and reached Brooks about 11 pm, perhaps earlier
because there was still a movie on the drive-in screen.
We unloaded Cindy, and I remember tying her up to the truck
box and the brome grass was up to her hips. We laid down
in the back of the truck – on some grass I pulled by hand –
and slept for about three hours, then drove into Calgary.
                                                     Annie'

(c)

No trees
around the house,
only the wind.
Only the January snow.
Only the summer sun.

Adam and Eve got drownded –
Who was left?

Stuart MacKinnon
The Intervals

We must say that these exist
since here are the names for them,
and we are aware of the intervals
between things, and the silences
between sounds.
PAUL VALERY, *Poems in the Rough*

■

In the long silence of the heart
longer than the wave reaching this shore
how did I come to this sad voice
how did I enter this dead space
sitting beside Sweetwater
staring at its shimmer
as if a stare could make it mean

Here beside the echo of the waves
Sweetwater song against my ears
and the shimmer far out
the birds move into
becoming black sunspots

On a map the lakes resemble
an empty womb

After ten years of travel
came here by chance
to sit beside this womb
of delicate cool inland lake
in the centre of the continent
and start to make a family and home

Another time and place I'm new to
this city   this narrow park
sixty feet wide of grass and cement
making a long corridor
between the hospital and prison
my back to careful traffic
on a bench between trees
in a niche like embankment sculpture
looking out to the lake
on a summer day of uncertain forecast
a short fresh wind off the lake
the gulls come down the city to
be held motionless
like a dream of paralysis

This park was built on old fortifications
that stick out under water like drowned cannon
I'm asking myself what holds me here
and how did I get here
living as usual
anywhere but in the present
treading air in an interval
a period of time between events
also intervale
I keep coming back to every lunch hour
soft rich place beside the river
on secure and comfortable ground

So many names for this state
so many meanings

                    interval
                    interregnum
                    hiatus
                    winter of the heart
                    halcyon days
                    lacuna
        they all express this gap I'm sitting in
            doing Lone Dog's winter count
                    trying to name the things
                        which interest me
                            trying to fit in
                                without damage

■

Eating lunch in cautious isolation
not wanting to be seen
trying to be a private man
in a public park
trying to look unapproachable
for whatever reason
afraid and defensive
wishing to be left alone
with my endless dreary speculations
about what I was waiting for
or why the sky colours the lake
or whether there are numbers
in the sky that order everything
beyond improvement or repair
a presence brushed my sleeve
then plucked it like a fish
and I looked up into a mouth that moved
to scramble sound into an urgent code
his ears plugged and wired
for sounds I couldn't make
and his light urgent wish
opened a small heavy hole
in the deepest part of my stomach

The nausea panic of helplessness
in the face of helplessness
the voiding   the fear
of having an uncontrolled wanderer in my body

A girl came from behind
and spoke into his hearing aid
reminding him he had just eaten
and didn't need my lunch
and he swayed abruptly off
leaving me stunned into the day
watching him wander off down the walk
dragging his keeper in the erratic wake
wishing I had talked to him
instead of looking to his nurse for help
could have offered him food
held his hand   shown each other
light on water   trees in wind
sticks held in the hand
up in the wind persuaded to be
some wind form
but I could only sit
like the deaf and dumb
of my adult world
whose questioning had made
objects of everything

There I was waiting for the new
thought or revelation or what
ever would come over me
give me feelings
or at least direct me to what
would take me out of this interval
of comatose seclusion
this mute took my by surprise

brought me back to water
held me to
the chemicals that rush fear
through the body   showed me
trees their hands in my flesh
wind going through the branches
of my lungs   the food
falling through everything
the chemical reactor

changing   pumping   driving
my nails and hair out
snapping crackling movement everywhere
worms air the ground
the strong
       brown
              body   we live on
                    the body

I went back to the lake every day
half wishing to see him again
turning over all the analogies
all the experiences   trying to find
the fear and the attraction
and I remembered Ruth
who told me how she
followed a waking dream
a walking death
her younger sister
simple from birth
lived with and cared for
that wayward body
all her younger life

I thought of Ruth
who took us into
times the memory rejects
the long dull waiting
those minds that society rejects
children   idiots   fools
who have no memory
must be remembered for
                who showed me
how to care for those who live
in their own imaginings
wandering in the body
             must know
how to survive such isolation
  must know such loneliness

■

I began to put together
times before I'd had this fear
once slumped in my chair
in front of the fire
exhausted after work
I was looking at a self portrait
Sally's optical colour flashes
went into a trance
and dreamed I was a simpleton
looked after by my sister
walking in a field
at the edge of the forest
maple trees moving rustling
in a heavy wind
the huge green lung
dropped into the atmosphere to writhe
and devour and make chemical change
I became a vegetable
without thoughts or fears
just happy perception and someone to follow
at a discreet distance
I was well looked after

Came out of the dream
very confused talking like
I could choose between dream and real
between being vegetable and human
decided to try the vegetable
and went to bed
woke up shortly
my feet numb
the numbness spread up my legs
like hemlock like comatose dread
if it got to my heart
I would die or be a paralyzed vegetable

Sat up scared
and talked myself down

      still
      heart
      be
      still

■

Something in the body
                          some small part
that could be expanded   spread
like a supreme imaginative act

Death   to spread it
rather   to let it spread
as it must be there
                          in the body
a small portion of each cell
of each moment   month   year
death
        in small doses our
        CATA / TONIC

To replace the fear of it
with the sense of
its nearness and certainty
the only absolute
we can be sure of

Side by side in the trance

Death / Imagine / Death

■

I kept returning to the embankment
that summer turning over my past
held there to an isometric
that simpleton had set in my head
envy of his freedom and security
fear of his outcast dependency
and saw in him the type
I had been taught to emulate
the pampered primitive
caught between reality and dream
the alien isolate
dependent on society
free in his restricted place with
the defence mechanism of withdrawal

where the imaginative vegetable is supreme
the poet is allowed easy access

■

Alone all that summer
and winter was the same as before
something fresh on the trees
would be an outrage
but lights were a reminder
in mid-winter days
the dark pause
xmas tree lights
all the power from
Churchill Falls
to run them
to remind us
of something
fresh
    on
      the
        bough

as usual
January and February
passed in a blue funk

■

Where do good thoughts come from
where do bad thoughts come from
out of mummy's tummy?

As Lucretius in The Nature of Things
  'What thing is it which meets us
    and frightens our minds when we
    are awake and under the influence
    of disease, and when we are buried
    in sleep'

Where does depression come from
is it the fear of death
or the fear of change
is it a defence mechanism
why do the eyes become dull
the voice listless
the breath rotten
the consciousness unable to grasp
meaning or value from the surroundings

there is that point in winter
when the weather controls us
and the earth seems dead
when rich Canadian physicians
go south to catch the first spring
and escape the dreadful pause
that old people die in
when suicides are plentiful
and prisoners stab each other
or strangle in sheets
like winding umbilical cords

■

Would it be better to
sit on the floor
in groups of 5 or 6
hunch our shoulders up
furrow brows
set the chin
discuss earnestly
the whole situation

Or would it be better to
slump in the overstuffed
leather covered chairs
of boardrooms
yawn and dawdle
scheming the while
and pulling some strategy

or why not mortgage
the two ancestral farms
sink the money in some lost
north of Kaladar silver mine
which would go bust
now seventy years later
the same farms buried
under sands at Picton

But wouldn't it be just as well
to go to sleep for two months
and wake up fresh
as if a new year
                a new person
    a new world
was coming down around the ears

If I knew
   what to do
I'd be so blue

don't you think

and be doing
something worthwhile

I've got enough
  just living
without staging
anyway I'm no strategist

■

There is this place

where   if you look
             above the trees
             you see more trees
             or land or rocks
             sometimes with
             water running
             down the side

there is this place

where   if you look
             above your roof
             you see
             more buildings
             and the
             occasional
             tree

Living in an intervale
        or crater city
is so different from flatland
        or flatsville flats
        where you see
nothing but sky above the trees or buildings

in the flat places
they build mounds
its hard to tell
a drumlin
from a mound
all the earth
moved and dumped
sometime or other

Besides mounds, there are walls and special sites, like this Malicet town on an intervale of the St. John river, as W.O. Raymond described it in 1905:

Medoctec possessed many local advantages; the hunting in the vicinity was excellent, the rivers abounded in salmon, sturgeon, trout and other fish, and the intervals were admirably adapted to the growth of Indian corn – which seems to have been raised there from time immemorial. The site of this ancient Maliseet town is a fine plateau extending back from the river about fifty rods, then descending to a lower interval, twenty rods wide, and again rising quite abruptly sixty or seventy feet to the upland. The spring freshet usually covers the lower interval and the elevated plateau then becomes an island. The spot is an exceedingly interesting one, but, unfortunately for the investigator, the soil has been so well cultivated by the hands of thrifty farmers that little remains to indicate the outlines of the old fortifications. It is impossible to determine with absolute certainty the position of the stockade, or of the large wigwam, or council chamber, and other features commonly found in Indian towns of that period.

The only place where the old breast-work is visible is along the south and east sides of the burial ground, where it is about two feet high. The burial ground has never been disturbed with the plough, the owners of the property having shown a proper regard for the spot as the resting place of the dead. It is, however, so thickly overgrown with hawthorn as to be a perfect jungle difficult to penetrate. Many holes have been dug there by relic hunters and seekers of buried treasure.

■

Going through the gap
noone gives you measure
me as a boy on a dust white road
cut between black ledge
that stopped the hum
of my eyes' travel

      Did not climb out
      but walked through
      as measure is not given
      but taken

The hand open to friends
and closed against oppression

      Once through
      the eyes travel in circles
      expanding to
      the always unfamiliar
      cold new

■

Certain habits began to fall away
    that winter after
      eyes resting
        on nothing
          in particular
            habits
      began to fall away
      falling asleep with my eyes open
      in front of a white field of snow

■

Something had happened to the
academy of fine ideas and general patterns
those forms behind things
invisible orders
running through things
the clothesline of god
or Plato or whoever
in the sky holding up
our menial delight
from another better world
these hierarchies began
to yaw slowly off
loosening then pitching off
categories   norms   excellencies
began to cake up
and flake off
in the reflection of his eyes
there in the blank field
the blank stare
        blank remembrance
I had been asking myself
was there an order behind things
under the appearance
looking for the pattern
and I knew there was no order
for him but the one his eyes made
no order no plan no end
and slowly it began to matter less
and I started throwing out second hand gear
from the academy of fine ideas

■

    As love
     pulls out old connections
rips up the latest plan and scatters families
        to new espousals
      our world is dismembering
    to strict phenomena
       and we are left
    to assemble pieces
    thrown from an impulsive dream crater

Repeat
solitude for order
let the gulls patch the sun
some day I may pick up the pieces
and lug them in a box across a field
If a bull charged me
I'd throw the box in his face
and he'd explode in four dimensions
like a depressurized fish in an ice cube

Anything to break the pose.

■

Not by any conscious act of will
can we inhabit tense
but must follow the drift
of interest or amusement
or necessity in consciousness
wandering
              wholly in the present
only by surprise
              stunned into awareness
forgetting for a moment past and future
living so close to things
that we forget time and are united
to the gross particulars

I would live there
but haven't the strength to fasten myself
to such a wandering wheel and live instead
these periods of dull interspace
away from the shock
until time gets heavy
and I pass it or shake it
by sleep by dream
by repeating this walk to the park
like a chant
or by changing houses jobs friends
living months of unrelation
until a new shock a new atrocity
a new lover offers me
that taste of living

■

While waiting to pick up on something
waiting for the new thing which would
come over me the new as usual
took my by surprise
                     out of this interval
this place in time of lineliness and isolation
slowly out to see the familiar
grow meaningful again
showing itself as having changed
in my absent minded presence
so as never to be the same way twice
showing myself to have changed
in its absence and never as before
see water move in light thru green trees
as another world to be in
protected from the destructiveness
of my own or others' failures.

■

Living in my head so long
my extreme isolation
                              my imaginings
that seem so far from other men's
such personal allegories that for a time
I even stopped speaking to my best friends
and was a childlike simpleton
looked after by one I love
and hadn't know this
until he began to lead me slowly out
with plenty of time to see
the soft rich place beside the lake
the intervale of comfort and security
the park in a city of walls
the middle class I belong to
                              all these things
we have invented to keep out fear
and control the unpredictable changes

I began this moving out
of my self preoccupation
lead by a mute simpleton
into spaces of the citizens

■

Walking on edge of the lake between traffic and water
in the narrow park between two lines of shade trees
walking on the edge of isolation
the stone wall of the prison at one end
at the other the stone wall of the hospital
following the heels of runners
who come to
stamp the ground
go down the corridor
in and out of sight
broken into frames between trunks
hand held for split second after second
all the motions of the runner
strung out like Muybridge for viewing
The roadsign which they pass
oscillates with harbour wind
and points toward a possible accident
probable as the wind which keeps it wound
kinetic as the cars it warns
of the accident which will supply
moving parts to the hospital
The same wind
expropriated by great windmills
on the hospital roof
goes to lungs that refuse it
to people on a classical mountain
an enormous blank wall
that no wind can move
and no sun can warm

∎

I have been taking lunches at the hospital
where Isadora plans the diet
She takes me through the meals
she plans for maximum sustenance
Going to meet her in the cafeteria
I pass through corridors of detention
the lake spreads its surface below me
where expensive pleasure boats
are play toys in a black sand box
At the end of each corridor
I enter the nexus
a room of identical doors
where passages meet
From each door a body may emerge
laid out on a giant roller skate
driven by a white nurse with starched spine
Always these small waiting
rooms full of decisions
doors without signs
only this halt to find direction
where none is given
this bland interval like the others

■

The hospital runs on principles of self sufficiency
the same ones my father deeded to his sons
four thousand people geared to independent functions
of emergency locked into a dependency without community
the building a germ factory like the bodies in it
where virile hybrids breed new plagues that must not spread
Change is the danger and must be ruled
where plague is a fire at sea
the whole building a prison ship
where the epidemic must run its course
and practitioners of germ warfare
hearing the fire in the next bunker
turn on auxiliary power
suck in air from the roof
or wait for accidents outside
to bring in moving parts

Nurse and doctor nurse and patient
love and donate their unwanted babies to charity
and study the psychology of dying
The quiet zone exudes from the masonry
and blooms in signs about the area
signs of the next expropriation
that the chief administrator plots
on graph paper gridded over the city map

I sit in the cafeteria with Isadora
watching her marriage come apart
and give my help that seems so slight
a thin mixture not on the menu
gruel containing equally small portions
of wisdom consolation and love
all my poor heart can raise
watered down with lots of talk

While here in another room
the Doukhabor women who started their hunger strike
four months ago in the prison
are being force fed intravenously
their fat sullen bodies now grown thin with defiance
kept alive by rubber hose and thin fluids
they alone will not swallow bureaucracy
who have defied the school system
and the government with their only weapon
the naked body its cast of shame
now lie naked before their enemies
food pressed into their veins

In my dream the Doukhabor women are coming
out between triumphal prison gates
facing the eastern morning light
in a long procession
                    They are dressed
in traditional Russian peasant's clothes
colourful and healthy and oversize
like the fat wooden Russian dolls
that have smaller dolls inside
and look hieratic and almost mummified
At the head of the procession
two women lead a great decorated bull
Perhaps they are celebrating a marriage
Perhaps in my dream it is the marriage
to the true society of men
the communal classless socialist society
going on without interruption

■

Dear Blair   April 21
Finally they did it — The prisoners tore up
the jail smashed the maximum security
and ripped the shit out of it — They've been
at it four days now and all the middle class
townspeople are scared shitless in case they
get out — I suppose they think the prisoners
will rape their wives and shoot up the town
— that's their nightmare the fear they live
with and suppress and are reminded of each
time they pass the pen because to them the
place is full of homicidal maniacs those vio-
lent ones from the lower classes just waiting to get at their wives or money or meat
choppers as if all the social anger and guilt
had been transferred to these men and
therefore they must be carrying all that
anger and they are — anyway it was an excellent uprising — They broke all the locking
mechanisms to the cells that run in radial
corridors off the central dome and they held
meetings under the dome where most of
the action took place including the beating
to death of two sex deviates who were cut
up with broken bottles in a sadism that was
not part of the main action — also they
smashed the chapels — All that hatred tearing down a medieval torture chamber and
partly because they knew that the new
prison they would be transferred to was a
modern torture chamber with electronic
locks and surveillance by closed circuit TV
and they didn't want it — It was the class
war sporadic and adventurist and futile but
for all that revolutionary — Four thousand
men eighty-eight hours under the dome
taking their collective vengeance on the
capitalist classes for a short while liberat-
ing the prison —
     Yours till we are all liberated
                              Stuart

The Halcyon

Olson   Eliot   Graves   the Greeks first
then Weston commenting on them
how to figure the rise and fall of states
the installation of a new king
or the change of any social order
work and rework myth

   Mythographers   historians   iconoclasts
   refurbish   erect   pull down
   the story remains the same
   not in itself permanent
   but what it refers to:
                Eternal change
                the too strict forms
                must give way

   In the year at winter's worst
   in the heart stunned
   after the end and before the beginning
   the worst part of change
   waiting to pick up threads

                Featherbedding it
                across the plains
                in northern winter

■

It's fall and the prisoners are being tried so humbly
The judge lists with bended ear
to limber up his justice
while twelve shackled prisoners hobble to dock
each one with a uniformed keeper
very well looked after
average age twenty
charged with murder during the riot
The judge is fat   the jury middle class respectable
prisoners lower class   twelve against twelve
that way man to man   easier to keep track
judge to have deciding vote
The spectators   myself among   sit in a circle
under the courthouse dome waiting to be let in
The judge lists with bended ear
to limber up his justice   lets go a few small arms
at the spectators to effect they must dress respectably
or not be admitted and they must show no
sympathy with nor solidarity with neither inside
not outside the prisoners   the courthouse
It's fall and the prisoners are being tried so humbly
I'm beginning to mumble and contemplate
making a disturbance
At lunch I take a walk on the deserted waterfront
in the abandoned shipyard where children
have chalked the walls with loud graffiti
The wind is getting up equinoxial
equal strength of day and night
equal pull of the dialectic
and blows me all the way back
to the courthouse for the afternoon session
complete with coffee breaks   and your honour
what I want to say is this:
                              If you stretched a cable
from the courthouse dome to the prison dome
and you hung these men by the neck from it
that would be about as obvious
as the way you're doing it now
also if the wind got up a little higher
the strain in this credibility gap
might pull down both your houses

■

COMA:
They keep punching my ass with these sedatives
or giving me pills   keep me high all the time
When I can't get some from the attendant
the others always have some
or else its in the diet
I'm beginning to mumble and rave
sitting in front of the gas fire
maybe its the smoke or

Coma dream   smoke good dope
up the tube   sucked up
into a roundness above the head
yet attached by a thread to my body
I'm really well taken care of
all these good people
my wife   the chief warden   the prime minister
they all have my best interest at heart
even given me this attendant
only he's really a spy
He's got the electrodes to my brain
looking like a harmless hearing aid
sometimes it give me shock treatment
sometimes it asks questions
like the next hit or the next assassination
the next cell meeting   the next riot
they would like me to start a riot
release me then catch the others
that's their dependency
muddy the stream then see where it comes out
put dye in one arm take it out the other

If it comes through then the body is sick
send it to the funny farm beyond help
If the dye stops then x-ray and excise
the organ that sequesters it
I wander in a sick body politic
                              homing   homing
my hair standing up to catch the breeze

People whose hair stands up are fanatic
you can tell a freak or fascist
or communist   their hair stands up
Eskimos too   they tell direction
by short hairs on the nape
Its a mind bender   I tell you
that raver   Hitler   a dye injected in Germany
homing device for Churchill's bombers
carrying Krupp fuses
but let Hitler cripple Russia first
to soften up the underbelly of Communism
then kill and divide Germany
and make plastic anarchy

The water supply is chlorinated and fluorinated
the state dieticians have put LSD in the bread
I wonder as I wander in the body politic
and I rave
become fanatic
dream this coma
take little trips
to the funny farm
start riots
in the pen

■

You who enter an interval
of time   of space   of music
letting the effort of generation
drop from your eyes and hands
Who enter a valley   a gap   a winter
to let all interest drop
Who enter unaware
the empty space between events
remember from one who knows it well
that your state of trance
is like standing in traffic
which blurs and blurs the vision
as you wait to cross to
subliminal glimpses

Take to yourself
the carelessness of simpletons
the stare of patient men gone snowblind
the limp persistence of water
the openhandedness of a grid
the protective slant of prisons
the antiseptic of hospitals

Take these qualities to yourself
as you sit like me by the lake
watching the wind thread the waves to discard
They will help you to survive
these minor passages coming out
on the other side with no baggage
and eyes unaccustomed to the light

■

Walk
    over the same ground
    again and again
Stand
    in moving water
try to stamp a path
        or cut a figure
you cannot walk the water down
but must drift helpless in the stream
loving and tentative
the movement of your body accomodating
not wishing to own or control
but to be helpless
pulling things together as they happen
and getting them all together occasionally

The permanence you seek
the order you wish to classify
lovely Heraklitos the first to ride chaos
seeing in change
        permanence
    in conflict
        rest
Harrassed T.S. Eliot the last to try
your voice over the moving water is desperate
and that the difference between
despair and helplessness

■

This yellow leaf on the water
This hand moving inside the wave
                              so helpless
Some ride
          some struggle
                        some close their eyes
                        and drown
Nothing to do with being passive or active
but with learning how to ride

■

I have rested by calm water
and seen the wind take up work
and fill my sight presently with waves

The quickness and the stillness
were of the same substance
and yet so various as to be a different thing
by offering different possibilities

I was looking for the changes
to anticipate some end
or make some pattern
and saw only a succession of
calm and movement
that made intervals

And looked at my life and yours
to see a simple likeness
tried only to look for common ground
on which we would be willing to build

The intervals are the silences that make sound distinct
    the stretch of pitch that makes harmonics
The intervals are the time of rest or privacy
    the space between the steps
    that take us to the future

Daphne Marlatt
Steveston

Imagine: a town

Imagine a town running
                 (smoothly?
a town running before a fire
canneries burning

              (do you see the shadow of charred stilts
on cool water? do you see enigmatic chance standing
just under the beam?

              He said they were playing cards in the
Chinese mess hall, he said it was dark (a hall? a shack.
they were all, crowded together on top of each other.
He said somebody accidentally knocked the oil lamp over, off
the edge

      where stilts are standing, Over the edge of the
dyke a river pours, uncalled for, unending:

                  where chance lurks
fishlike, shadows the underside of pilings, calling up his hall
the bodies of men & fish corpse piled on top of each other (residue
time is, the delta) rot, an endless waste the trucks of production
grind to juice, driving through

                 smears, blood smears in the dark
dirt) this marshland silt no graveyard can exist in but water swills,
endlessly out of itself to the mouth

                  ringed with residue, where
chance flicks his tail & swims, through.

Imperial Cannery, 1913

Standing inside the door (the river ...) how shadow lies
just inside the cannery floor, sun, pouring down outside
the river streaming slow, slow, by. Now she feels old enough,
now she is wearing her long print dress & leaning into the
threshold, waiting for work, the wheel that time is, Whose hands
are standing still, hers, empty, Whose friends also surround her,
waiting, waiting all morning for the fish to come. Nothing moves
but occasional strands of long hair the subtle wind is lifting,
up off the river, the Fraser, mouth of the Fraser here where it
debouches, into marsh, delta, swirling around & past those
pilings of the cannery wharf they are standing on, muddy &
pale grey teeming, invisible fish ...

                               Now she is old enough to be her
mother inside, working, with the smallest one standing by her skirt
in grubby dress, & the blood streams down the wooden cutting board
as the 'iron chink' (that's what they call it) beheads each fish ...

Now she is old enough for the wheel's turn, she is feeling her
body in its light dress wind blows thru, as past the faces of
her friends, likewise silent, impassive. Wind blows thru
those open doors (two) because, in the dark where machines are,
& the cans, & the steam, & a cavern of men with rolled up
sleeves & straw hats, & men in oilcloth slickers spattered with
fish gut, beyond & across the corner of that dark stands
another door, & the sail of a boat crossing the river, wind,
wind ... An open door, where men unload their hauls of fish, the
collector's boat, float, sliding one, a hundred, on top of another,
their own scale grease that keeps them alive in sea they're
taken from to dry, in open sun on an open dock.

But she is in her
element, dreaming of sails, her father's, or a friend's son, at the
Imperial which owns their boat, their net, their debt. But the
Fraser gives of itself, incessantly, rich (so the dream goes),
& wooden houses jammed on pilings close together, leaning, with
wooden walks & muddy alleys, laundry, & the dry marsh grass that
stutters out of silt the dykes retain, from a flowing
ever eroding & running river ...

dreaming, of fabric she saw at Walker's Emporium, & the ribbon. A
woman of means she dreams, barefoot on the dock in the wind, leaning
into her threshold of work, machines, the wheel that keeps turning
turning, out of its wooden sleeve, the blade with teeth marked:
for marriage, for birth, for death.

Pour, pour

from its bank) this river is rivering urgency, roar
(goku, goku) thru any hole, like boats race tide a millrace, as,
the possible entry of this channel for, invisible under their hulls
& flying heels, the fish re-enter time, racing north of Roberts Bank
past Albion Dyke, then Woodward Reach opposite Woodward Landing
(where the ferry ran) by Woodward Slough, then Gravesend Reach &
City Reach the river proper lies, past any tidal reach (renew) fish
seek their source, which is, their proper place to die ...

'This river is
alive,' he says, crippled fisherman on the radio watching water
swollen with its filth, with sewage, milldirt, strain at the sandbag
dyke, at its container, uncontainable, irrational (hence renewable)
creature, swelling up & birthing, huge, past all their plans & plants,
its urgency to meet the sea where men go, when they are able, like the
fish. It eddies too, backwater Hong Wo, where (unable) moss
shackles an abandoned roof, or marsh grass thick with seed heads
silent (bunkhouse) into a wind live off the river sun is scouring,
walk, a wall will be, silent as light-rimmed wood, knowing what?
evidence?

gaunt, a face glimpsed from behind tatter windowhanging
keeps, he keeps their store (his, haunt) locked dust, its stilled clock
barely visible, shelves still stocked, in part, in part vacant-eyed,
he stares trying not to be seen, to see, he is the visible remnant
of time's push, here where it eddies back on his suspicion, under the
fencedup place he keeps his dog, back of the dock, this place (source)
he haunts, his bark, or its, invisible guardian of old receipts,
accounts not rendered, months yellowing into irrelevant years (some
seven in quick succession, glancing, like light off water no one
registers, the way tide swells up under these pilings where the tag ends
of his mind keep, Hong Wo's, good luck chips, echoing down the galvanized
floor of wash tank across the way, in back of what was once, one, two,
three, four, company, source of (need as cash) or, a kind of company account
no hand skims now, closing in on this life, this, or this, foreclosed at
dusk now, opening the door he wanders out to sit, leaning his chair
against the wall & contemplating closedup house boards, a sweltering
mattress or the few remaining cards: as visages, his vision is accretion
uncountable (is he? accountable?) or facing mountains he can't see, wires,
& the roar of Richmond skyline (money), only the falsefront silhouette
'west' is occupies his mind, disused (opportune) broccoli box tide swells &
moves, this way or that, but always to cast up finally in the muck low
tide shallows, or the last spasm a visible body leaves, some seed as
imprint or, continuance, continuing to pour/down as light, or time,
this town down stream its own downpour ...

Moon

       half moon, hot night. water seeping up, wetting
island dirt. It's river, rank odour of river mud banks, the
strait, the sea. That smell of night come lightly on the body of
the earth's heat, full of the day

                    It's stagnant ditch water, drainage
gathering scum, Lulu Island, dyked off from the sea.

                          Half moon,
Saturday night, hot June: already would have shot the season in
all up & down her banks a sound of cedar corks crescending
over the gunnels of boats, paid out by hand, at 6, on Sunday night,
the week begins. Night before, ten thousand people pack the town, a
crush, on the board sidewalks' eight-foot planks, the taverns'
rustle of silk, boots. boots upstairs. pitcher of water blood hot,
heat trapt up in those gable rooms, in a gambling eye ...

White as the moon, who was she? apart from the different dreams they
had, in smoke & whisky, & then the Indians, Chinese, Japanese unknown
in numbered houses. But mostly those her like up from San Francisco,
turning in the aura of a silk-pleated shade those white arms
suddenly lifted, naked, Lulu. Lulu Sweet's namesake this Island,
spawning in the dive of fisherman kids under the walk for change that
spills from tight & multiple pockets of the packers. Scotch-English,
Phoenix, Colonial, Paramount, this moon-crazed industry (you hear that
splash at night of nets?), this town ...

Now so quiet only frogs sing in ditches soon to be covered as per
housing development, each internal room focused on a further internal
screen, whose smaller & smaller ponds of thought these 'channels' bring

    In from the Outside, where the night lives, this spring, this
moon as every spring: freshet, & the salmon churning black waters,
darker depths.

A few people drink in the Steveston, a few
young men: stopt up, burning, slow, nowhere to go, no crowds to
light, no strange women, no gambling games, no risk. Except the
occasional storm outside, the rare failure of guaranteed equipment,
the unexplained accident

                as shipwreck, or, only the *smaller* packers
forced out, bought up.

            This corporate growth that monopolizes
the sun. moon & tide, fish-run. So they see nothing remarkable
in this, they know it like the back of their hands on a familiar
table, like fish conveyed by belt to the steady chopping of steel
blades. Beer to lips, end of a shift, end of another week. It
sucks them dry, these men soaking in their beer (so many thousand
cans today), these women in white, tired, or wearily hopeful, drained
by the ditches of their unsatisfied lives.

Steveston as you find it:

                           multiplicity simply there: the physical matter of
the place (what matters) meaning, don't get theoretical now, the cannery.

It's been raining, or it's wet. Shines everywhere a slick on the surface of
things wet gumboots walk over, fish heads & other remnants of sub/ or
marine life, brought up from under. Reduced to the status of things hands
lop the fins off, behead, tail, tossed, this matter that doesn't matter,
into a vat or more correctly box the forklifts will move, where they swim,
flat of eye – deathless that meaningless stare, 'fisheye' (is it only
dead we recognize them?) in a crimson sauce of their own blood.

                                        We orient
always toward the head, & eyes (*e*yes) as knowing, & knowing us, or what we do.
But these, this, is 'harvest'. These are the subhuman facets of life we the
town (& all that is urban, urbane, our glittering table service, our white
wine, the sauces we pickle it with, or ourselves), live off. These torsos.
& we throw the heads away. Or a truck passes by, loaded with offal for what
we also raise to kill, mink up the valley.

                              That's not it. It's wet,
& there's a fish smell. There's a subhuman, sub/marine aura to things. The
cavernous 'fresh fish' shed filled with water, with wet bodies of dead fish,
in thousands, wet aprons & gloves of warm bodies whose hands expertly trim,
cut, fillet, pack these bodies reduced to non-bodies, nonsensate food *these*
bodies ache from, feet in gumboots on wet cement, arms moving, hands, cold
blowing in from open doors facing the river, whose ears dull from, the in-
sensate noise of machinery, of forklifts, of grinding & washing, of conveyor
belt. Put on an extra sweater, wear long underwear against the damp that
creeps up from this asphalt, from this death that must be kept cool, fresh.

'DISINFECT YOUR GLOVES BEFORE RESUMING WORK.'

That no other corpus work within it. Kept at the freshest, at the very point of
mutable life, diverting, into death. To be steamed in cans, or baked, frozen in
fillets, packaged sterile for the bacteria of living bodies to assimilate. break
down. Pacific Ocean flesh.

No, that's not it. There's a dailiness these lives revolve around, also immersed.
Shifts, from seven to four or otherwise. Half an hour for lunch. & a long
paperwrapt & tied form outside the lunchroom, keeping cool. 'til shift's
end & the fridge, supper, bed. 'my life', etc.

'You leave 2 minutes after 4,
& not before, you understand? Two minutes after.' Two minutes, as if that,
together with the sardine cans for ashtray, made all the difference. Which is,
simply, as two Japanese women sit, relaxing with their fifteen minute coffee
out of thermos, more likely hot soup, one rearranges the chrysanthemums, red &
yellow, she placed in an empty can on their table this morning when the day
began. Or more directly how in 'fresh fish' the lunchrooms, men's & women's,
face over an expanse of roof with flowerboxes even, river & the delta, Ladner,
space. & remain spacious, time turned calendar of kimona'd beauty, kneeling,
on the wall. While in the cannery close to wharfedge they face north,
backed by old wooden lockers to the door: DO NOT SPIT IN THE GARBAGE. USE THE
TOILETS. & here they flood in together, giggling, rummaging thru bags,
eating grapes, girlish even ('I've worked here 20 years') under severe
green kerchief like Italian peasants, except that they are mostly Japanese,
plunked under a delicate mobile of Japanese ribbon fish in their gumboots
& socks. Break, from routine, with the ease of tired bodies laughing,
for what? 'It's life.' *Their* life?

Or how the plant packs their lives, chopping
off the hours, contains *them* as it contains first aid, toilets, beds, the
vestige of a self-contained life in this small house back of the carpentry
shed, where two woodburners are littered with pots & hot plates, & the table
still bears its current pattern of dominoes. Where a nude on the wall glints
kittenish at one of the two small rooms inside, each with iron bed. Some
sleeping place between shifts? Dark. Housing wet dreams, pale beside the
clank of forklift, supply truck, welding shed.

It's a mis-step, this quiet gap on everyone else's shift, when you're off,
when accidental gravel rattles loud on the wooden walk. wan sun. coffee,
gone cold. There's a surface skin of the familiar, familial. Running into
shadow, where old socks, someone else's intimate things, call up the fishy
odour of cunt, of lamp black in the old days you could hear them screwing
behind their door (cardboard), & even the kitchen still exists to pull you
back in, to smallness, a smell of coal, the aura of oil, of what comes up
from under, sleeping – nets, wet still from riverbottom, & the fish.

This darker seam that slips underneath the coppery gleam of all those cans stacked
flat after flat, waiting transfer. Men. & Women. Empty familiar lunchroom,
& the dream, pounding with the pound of machinery under mountains of empty packer
pens at night, the endless (white) stream of flesh passing under the knives,
To be given up, gone, in a great bleeding jet, into that other (working) world.

How it goes

Men sleeping, lives, or lives sleeping, doors. On Moncton, in the
store window, a pall draped placard reads:

<blockquote>
In Memoriam

Steveston Post Office

Doors closed

May 13th 1972
</blockquote>

Women wend their way past, if they do,
unconcerned (it flows) or crossing doors, grocery, cannery, library floors,
'you can't hear yourself think with all that noise', they're tearing up the
pavement on Number One again. They continue, as if. it wasn't so long ago
they changed direction, roads, leaving sea & moving inland, inroads to a
heart that changes. Monopoly. 'The kids grow up & go elsewhere', she said,
not fishing, not limited to that, or limited, how the company pays, & she
stays. Somewhere, children keep growing up baseball heroes, while sun slowly
lightens the doctor's floor, behind blinds, behind history, a facade
salvaged & rendered useful, or the old houses back of Steves place,
shacks groaning awry in wind, into cow muck, into canary grass ...

the slap slap continues as a clock ticks somewhere on Moncton
& she comes home to the empty house ...

May day May day May day. He called Pan.
She should have cut the grass. Yesterday. He shouldn't have painted the house.
Yesterday. Yesterday was fine. & now the demolition crew, a church radio
floating off somewhere in the blue, while morning, eternal morning twines
weed, bindweed, creeps in the empty door at noon. At noon, 'maybe get a few
hours rest', they said, they sent her home.

'Distress.' How it continues.
Maybe it was, she thinks, maybe it might have been, a packer leaving the
Gulf Oil barge, crowd of fish boxes, silver, riding the sun. late afternoon,
8 men. 7 to help. They said he could ... Or later, 'you can sleep
all the way up to Bull Harbour if you want,' his chipt blue mug sliding
across the cabin floor, but, the way he wore his shirt, collar up against those
small hairs of his back, twisted somehow, stooped. They knew. Riding waves
or rising, into them, to the occasion. Heroism is not confined to the
sea. A pain, a pain rising & no one ...

'Distress signal should not be used where Urgency signal will do.' & so,
mouth shut, silent, falling into the sea – why won't they cry out? Doors
close. & she is haunted by it, as she crosses, into shadow, any silent
sunny street.

Sea Trek, etc.

                      trickle of broken hose. old netting, sacking, rope.
paint everywhere. penboards on end & painted silver. poles with
bells to be fitted, new springs & line. the sound of a boat
rubbing against tire, whisper of rope, shift across rope as a
boat lifts or falls.

                 Sea Trek, Elma K, Miss Nikko 70, ready,
day after day copper painted & caulked & overhauled, now they
wait, feeling that suck in green & oily shallows, feeling
afternoon leaf so close at hand, & late (derisive, clucking of
a gull domestic, finally) they wait, for headway out to the open
seas/ the open season, current, storm: & fish.

Low Tide. A beached vessel,

small grey gillnetter, chained to the
dock so close in to shore she's high & dry on rocks, angularly
beached, bleached, like some dying fish.

Where nothing belongs
in all this absent morning, only sun who owns these shells of
cannery housing, these unused footbridges, these brambles whose fruit
no one picks. Silent boats. Docks serving only sun, & wind off the
open waters. Moving. Down the track come 3 boys idle, looking for
some – Wow, a boat.

Her sullen cabin's locked, but two of them
violate a side window. Hey, a searchlight! Does it work? Look at
this! An empty bottle, flung in glittering arc across the sun,
smashes into a thousand bits.

The third, jimmying her door, Hey you guys, is there a metal
pipe in there? If you find a metal pipe I could smash every door
in the place.

The place? These kids, who live by the sea & know
nothing of boats. But orders, orders of power, of hoarded wealth.
Insistent, hey you guys, to break in on what the others are earnestly
engaged in: Somebody's pants! Got any money? Look, batteries,
gasoline, a licence – I could be a driver of a boat. Hey, cool!
this is a masterkey you know, it'll open up that door.

Inscrutably closed, she allows no keys to hold, nothing so easy –
as the fear somebody's beating somebody to it, every minute:
Hold this, hurry, I can rip the door off.

An older man, who's
walking down the tracks toward the Esso dock, anonymously watching,
stops at that. With voice of authority: Boys, you're not supposed
to be on there!

Sudden pause. Not on this boat?

No sir, not on any boat. Silence while they try it on for size,
unwilling. If the patrolman comes along you'll be in trouble.
Then he, unwilling to meet their eyes, walks off.

There's a lull, like a momentary cloud, an anxious thought. Is that
the patrol boat? Naaw, he's kidding. Come on!

Back to the joyous act of 'making' her, their secret catch.

End of Cannery Channel

Trolling bells, hammering. A storm of bells as the hammering
increases. Bird song. Grass smell. On the floats a litter
of corks, paint, packing cases, rags, freshly painted pen boards.
Tatters of net. raindrenched to the dock. And, at the end,
a clean looking troller, starboard pole dropped flat. Two men
bent over, replacing rusty springs & talking with a third who's
looking on. Who glances at my notebook.

'Are you going to raise the pole? I'd like to watch!'

'She wants to watch! (Laughing, he says something in Japanese
to the other two.) You gonna *help*?'

'Sure. I'll help you!'

'I'm kidding. These are heavy poles!'

'How heavy?'

'Well, flat on the wharf she's 200 pounds easy. Once you get her
to a 45 degree angle one man can lift, but down she takes 3 men!'

Water laps softly against the hull. There's a curious backwater
stillness to their work.

'Hot day huh? You want something to drink? (The others laugh.)
You wanna beer? We give you beer & maybe you dance for us eh?
Charlie get her a drink!'

'No, no I don't dance! The older man offers a sunwarm coke,
simply, as if disregarding the other's comments. 'Thanks!
& goes back to his work. 'Those springs are for the bells?
when you get a bite?'

He's leaning against the sawhorse wondering what I want. 'Yes, sure,
you married?'

'No!'

'Hippie?'

'No. Why?'

'Why not? Hippie's okay. Take me, I work hard & then go home to
the same old pork chop every night, you know what I mean? But you,
you have variety. Turkey one night, beef the next. Maybe try a
little fish eh?' (nudging the others)

I'm clearly a woman on their float. Too weak to lift the pole,
old enough to have taste — 'you know what I mean?' He eyes me
across the rift of language, race, & sex. Should I go?

Laughs suddenly, calls something in Japanese. They've tightened in
the last spring. Water reflects light off the underside of the
crosspiece (white) the pole will rise into. Suddenly mobilized,
they board her. Three men pulling on ropes, heave, grunt, call.
The boat shifts under lifting weight. Higher, she's pulling in,
close to the mast. Two hold, while he climbs up & hammers the
metal brace into place, grins down:

'See what it's like?'

In time

how the river washes them bare, roots trees
put down, knotted & twining into the wash of the Gulf, tidal, in, in & out
to the mouth, the gulf all trees, roots, clumps & knottings of men's nets
wash out to. Washing from east to west, how the river flows, washing its
filth downstream & silting islands of work men dredge their channels thru,
grassland, sedge. The work it takes to keep men busy, dredge at it, all
day long to keep a channel thru, street, straight thru (west) to ...

This chugging of an Easthope moving east to west, waiving sandbar, mudflat,
thru marsh you can't see past, as earlier steamer for Mrs Steves, 'But ma'am
no one lives there!' To be made *here*, island of grass seen as pasturage,
dairy farm. & then an island settlement, a settlement mentality that
settles down a street that doesn't go straight thru, pacing the river's
winding edge, that sez oblivious, good soil here we'll put our roots down.
And the river runs away with them, flood, storm, all manner of lost
belongings gone, anchorless on out to sea ...

The edge, the edge. Settled by it. Camped rather. Cluster of
fishing shacks temporary as those Japanese who slept on boats arriving, each
season, for the fish, to stay, stray into settlement, believing still they were
only here this year, sending money home & staying on to the next, & the next,
& the natives, whose longtime summer ground this was, coming to fish, whole
bands whose women & children end by working the canneries, staying in Indian
tenements, & it all settles down into an order of orders, the Chinese
tyee boss, & the cans hammered out by his men, orders of cash handed down
thru the messhall, the gambling & fires, fire & flood.

Always on the edge of, a Gulf where the river runs. West. by East/hope,
the push to 'make it', that leap into the end of pain, struggle, into 'settling
down', finally, into cash as, security. But it continues, this westward drift.
Islands of it moving west, 1000 feet per century. & this is not the end,
this accumulation along the way, deposits (in a bank, in the Richmond
Credit Union, in shares in BC Packers, in) a town whose main street moves,
as Manoah did, from Moncton New Brunswick, west, in a vision of telephone
poles, wires, cement. A straight line from east to west, from farm at its
eastern end, to Steveston Hotel, knife in teeth, Canada Fish.

                                                                    Shadowy, this
piratical emblem of another era. Boomtown. Dream of seizing silver wealth that
swims, & fixing it in solid ground, land, home. A mis-reading of the river's
push. Now Moncton Street walks a straight line that begins & ends. Never a
river, not even at season's peak or its end, tho it returns, at moments of,
it begins & ends, the day. The school day for instance when they stand in
2's & 3's with bicycles by the Marine Grocery. At times Christine's cafe is
almost full & the hardware does a running business, but no one runs
& the street does not flow. They have coffee at certain times of the day,
they meet, the fisheries officials, truckers, & men off their boats repairing,
overhauling, come up to warm themselves on their way to the bank. These
individual lives, discrete, closed off from one another, but known &
recognized. Islands of men the day weaves its way thru. Going someplace?
A store with no name, bales of net in the door. Stores for no end, the unused
highball glasses no one buys. Stores begin & end, small personable lairs,
'Tom's TV moved to Minamoru' up island where the tracts go – where the tracks
went farms used to lie, with their strawberry pickers & cranberry bogs on fire,
razed now to smoking inland freeway & North Arm plants ...

                                   Is there a gap? There is discontinuity as Moncton,
cowled in its quiet normalcy, intends a straight line the health inspector's
Packard drives down, & he unfolds, huge, & climbs out & crosses into Christine's.
& the fishermen sit with elbows on the counter, sipping coffee & talking, or
not talking, & nod. & the fisheries men greet him, & the truckers know him,
& Christine who is small & not Christine, who is quiet & Chinese, smiles &
brings him coffee as he packs himself, somehow, into the booth. Have you
seen his brother? he has a twin, the trucker sez, just as huge.

Always there is this shadow, long, that underlies the street & twins it,
running it to ground. As the river, at Atlas camp, throws up sand that cuts
the line Moncton extends (in mind) to the end. A line that lies, like
Moncton straight ahead, ignores this shadow that wavers & wanders, collecting
islands of lives, leaves them stranded or suddenly, after some years visible as,
time passing, picking stucco off the wall outside Hiro's, or drinking pop &
trading bubblegum cards. It lengthens slowly around them, slanting past Island
Cleaners, past the Richmond pool hall, past River Radio. Puddles, clouds
shining in them. So that this air of establishment, this density that is
cementblock Steveston Hardware or the old brick DRUGS now L & L Discount,
settles in the unseeing eyes of the old man in the pool hall, awash in beer &
sentiment, into history, into what he clings to now as evidence (in time –
of 'his' story.

Work

Glass of water on a hot day, at the counter. Water or sevenup.
Christine's: hotter than the street. Elbows on counter in quiet
solitude, locked into singleness the highboned profile of his face,
nevertheless like theirs flushed by the sun, declares *Fraser Princess*
tied up at floats some mile away, idle with the other boats. Now
fishing day's cut to one a week for sockeye. Thursday. Middle of
August almost.

Hello. His handshake lingers into holding-
hands – I'm pleased to see you – as he slides into the booth –
How are you? – squeezing my palm.

Last seen on the docks, fisherman of
consequence, quiet in the knowledge of his gear, his sons, their mutual
help, his years' experience here & in the world, as union executive,
salted always with their evacuation & return. The bitter seed of it
simply his protest, No I fish ... I handled *some* of their affairs,
that's all.

Whose invisibility stalks beside him like that
second skin his boat, appropriate to his dimensions, source & home.
Despite a house furnished with cannery pay, his wife's domain. But his,
at sea a tight & familiar space that's known, the way the poles are
set, how well she handles given uncertain weather; given fuel, a reliable
engine, she'd travel to Japan & back. No, it's the force or wake she
leaves, her cut of displaced water down the channel: It's the power to
motion, to *move* ...

Who will insist (so are you married? no? how's this?
patting my crotch) my presence haunts the dock, for what other reason
but these fishermen who cut the water of the channel proudly with their
boats, Cut, with a powerful motion, thru the weight of all that
surrounds them, on out to sea ...

Vision. Seen by them
as sexual obsession? Who, hands on the wheel, are driven by the
necessity of fishing, noise & confusion of gear, fish & the boat itself
nothing more than hard work, over & over.

But still, his hand pushing
down there, the teasing smile, 'Next time I fish West Coast I take you
with me eh?' that persists, that isn't meant to tease but to imply ...

                                        No, it's an old
dream my hair, my body happen to fit: the incarnate goal of all
that's *out there,* given birth in crowded ghetto conditions,
necessity to work up out of that mass, the pressure always ('after
the war they wouldn't even rent a house to us') to feel what one
man can do, where he can go ...

But then, he's 70, & they talk, the men in their coffee room on the
wharf, over dominoes & flower cards, of sex & young girls ('who's
your new girlfriend, Charlie?') of the hippies tied to government
wharf, what they'd be like, those free young ones who don't, it seems,
have to work.

                    (does he see me as one of them? 'Come down to my boat
Saturday – I'll give you a salmon.' What can I give in return?

                         That I persist, also, in seeing *them,* these men,

who are cut down to one day a week: their technology too great for
the crop to bear, $600 worth in one day off one boat. The persistence
that has always in the industry characterized them. He *knows* he's an
expert fisherman, tho deprecates, 'Oh one day a week's easier for an
old man like me.' But idle, how strange that idleness sits on one
given to work – A glass of water, a glass of sevenup, in town, at a
cafe counter. So familiar it's boring. But for the dream that surfaces
when the young woman from *out there* walks in, with whom, momentarily,
over a hamburger & a glass of water, he connects.

'Slave of the canneries'

> dipping into his album, fisherman's
oldest son. Beached in the mountains. Raised on fish to
fish. As young boatpuller seasick ('my dad, he used to get so
mad at me he'd dump me on the wharf'), on solid ground:

Reifel Sanctuary: photos of this man with birds, geese,
tucked under one arm. Working white millionaire's ground
with care, for flood gates, trees' growth, observation tower.
Photos of the family house, the family 'his' he worked for.
His also, *Lone Eagle*, must go fishing to support, age 23,
nine brothers & sisters & the grandmother whose friend ('she
knew a little bit about such things') delivered them in *this*
house on the drainage canal, company-owned, on pilings so
eaten away they have to jack it with a shingle bolt from
salvaged logs.

> Stench of rotting cannery offal floating by,
shit house seepage from these company houses crammed side by side,
footbridges they'd wheel their netcarts over, by ditches drained
by tide. Drainage of this island salvaged out of saltmarsh, these
people drained, resting in their barely salvaged houses where
rats skitter, night, eat at nets drying upstairs the hunger of
eleven people rests on:

> grace of company loans (debt), of split
cabbage salvaged from slightly wealthier Japanese farms, 'our diet –
rice, salted fish, & vegetables,' day in, day out ('I still like
salted fish'), survival as the *minimum* requirement, nothing more.
hoped for. given the limits (sawmill, farm, or fish ...

These mountains now,
New Denver, rise up round a slow lake windblown sometimes, seeming to
go nowhere. By Carpenter Creek, Orchard so humanly overgrown, a
ghetto for evacuees: small shacks again crammed side by side,
brown shingled this time, fronting the lake. Two thousand Japanese
in a few square blocks. Uprooted from the flats, the muddy river,
saltwind. Trucked in or deported by train to landlocked winter
where the clear air, frozen water's good for TB they say
(hemorrhaged in Hastings Park building human pens), 'It was a
good experience.' 'How can you say that?' 'For the next generation.
Look at my daughter, she's a pharmacist!'

And so curiously pulled out of
the delta's restraining ring of debt broken by mass theft
(seizure at government level), these impoverished 'enemies of
the state', transplanted & forced into new growth, shed a
mass of memoirs that evidence their real estate the four
walls testify to, over the years, room after room added, still
not finished.

To the man who gardens, cares for
the old folks' home, caretaker of the ghetto water tower (invisible
geese under one arm), marker of past loves & past faces gone
with a river cresting, Immoveably settled here like some crustacean
in this valley where nothing runs to sea except the water, 'one of
the few remaining lakes of BC ... sufficiently pure & unpolluted'
to drink from / To: the pool, the still lake of our muddy &
intermingled present.

Not to be taken

from Lum Poy's back door facing due
west across an abandoned field (150 acres of good soil 'assembled
& sold by Al Austin') beyond the dyke which humps hiding marsh
(you can hear visiting wild geese there), hidden, channel markers &
the jetty, only: mountains of Island visible in all that fire dusking
deeper & deeper tongues of scarlet purple grey — this Gulf pour,
into a cavernous mouth of flame & wind & water westward, ruffling skin
heat caressed by dew start underfoot, in seed grass, rank wild
water smell of

River, rolling out of the darker east, tide turn & wind.
We hesitate on the brink of sinking, ourselves, to this cracked & heat-
hugged clay, to

marsh gas the flicker of dead grass in water, swamp,
in all those small farms surrounded by ditches, road ditches, hand-
(gone, as ghost) dug ditches — 'In those days drinking water was delivered
by wagon but they used ditch water for washing' their rags, now clay off
hands, translated by the tyee boss as anonymous numbers 'these men (who)
had to work 3 years to pay off their passage money' 'were used by the
municipality to dig ditches'. A pool of labour seeping into the land as
cannery workers, coolie gangs, saving to own some few acres of solid
ground

despite the indestructible rot of vegetable matter, a mouldering
telephone book, somebody's clothing. Hands, it changes. Boughtup land,
sediment 10,000 feet of, wild clay furrows cracked in spring since 1968
no irrigation, this side of (the dyke) recurrent freshet, muddy & turbulent
(shaking of blue veins in a withered wrist

(not to be, NOT TO BE

in the dust, in the dust & dank of a boardedup house sun never lights
nor wind blows thru these windows dark against the day's heat lingering
still, as piss-fed grass this house is dead to, deaf the stalls of
adjoining barn a single pried door leads into

                                              shadow bowls on a
broken chair, a solitary corner for someone's hurried mouthful gulped
by nightfallen fields already abandoned in prevision, the 'last'
sunset, a 'last' swallow soaring above the day's field, salvaged, tilled &
handpicked into fragile baskets of claydust, wrinkle eyes, sore back,
Looking up, under cornhusk & bambooslatted coolie hat at the monster
machine beating down the ditch, sucking, widening, raising the levee,
piledriver-&-dredge progress shoring familial fields their backs ache from,
their lives

                              (NOT TO BE TAKEN

For this was 'flat prairie – good redtop grass,' This was 'swampy –
reeds, flags, low willows.' A host of mosquitoes, dragonflies, small
crickets

        where no one stands

                        empty, waiting the bulldozer tracts,
demolition, scaffolding & sewer drains, the ript denuded soil patches
of artificial grass will cover, like burial plots.

        '35 acres assembled & sold by Al Austin'

                                    Afloat in a welter of
facts they left: Christmas cards in English from Chinese friends, Sunday
School biblical pictures, calendar, odd socks, receipts, broken crockery,
a blue bottle ... a small hexagonal blue bottle with faded label, Chinese,
badly printed doctor's face. Uncorkt, a last lingering residue of some
red liquid, aromatic & strong as horse liminent.

                                This residue
faint as marsh gas over the soil, soiled, in blue raised letters down
one side, NOT TO BE TAKEN: a residue of pain, dug into the land.

Finn Road

'Seems like, with men around, you're always at the stove.'
Making cabbage rolls, something that keeps in a slow oven when
the boys come back, late, from fishing. It's her day off. She
went to town to pay the bills, 'somebody's got to look after that.'
But tomorrow she'll be up when the tide's full, at 3 or 4 in the
morning, down to Finn Slough where her boat's moored. Been out
fishing for 20 years now. And walks, from counter to stove, with a
roll.

It's a hot day, sultry, rain spit in the air.
There's cotton laid out on the kitchen table, a pattern. 'Making
a housecoat,' something cool to wear when it gets humid. 'Seems
like, whenever it's strawberry & haymaking time, there's rain.'

A by-channel; a small backwater:

                                        slough, Finn Slough (or Gilmour,
by Gilmour Island), slough for sale as 'deep sea frontage',
has been always, simply, backwater clutch of shacks, floats,
sheds: a swamp & dusty marsh grass sheltering mosquito boats,
small gillnetters & other vessels in this amphibious place,
half earth half water, half river half sea, tide fills, swiftly,
pushing muddy fingers into timbers of the float, crawling round
pilings & rushes, glinting up a web of net stranding float where
a man & a woman bend, knotting holes deadheads & other refuse a murky
river roils, have torn, ripped, & otherwise scorned, sometimes from
leadline to cork ...
                                        The slow effort of
this people's morning: rise with predawn birdsong & coffee
stretching stiffer & stiffer bones, pack lunch, pad past the
cloistered silence of tv, crunch of gravel, drive (green Pinto)
down to where their boats lie, light filtering immense
vegetation.

                Check fuel, untie & start the engine ('a 7 Easthope
& a 15, wasn't it a 15 Easthope they had too? They thought they really
had something on the go – now when they look back they think it's a
joke, you know, why, have we actually been fishing with those?'

'That was the onetime king engine' on this coast, days when
nobody had any money, they bought a used car engine for two bucks,
had it delivered down to the slough, the poor

                                        shelter of swamp
houses, float ('when I look at it now it looks like a summer cabin')
under the lee of a dyke Finnish squatters & other folk whose lives
are inextricably tied with the tide that inundates their day, their
time measured only by: this sucking at vegetal silence swallows shred,
from the boom of idle boats, from the ridgepole of shadowy netshed
jets drone: this land up for deep sea frontage ('oh yes, it'll be
freighters & cement scow, barges & containerized shipping all the
way up to New Westminister,
                        you can't stop progress, can you?'

How *accept* its creeping up?
like a disease, like time, the tide they still know how to run,
with it, up under ('remember how your net got wrapped & rolled?')
that barge, danger at dark or fog, still after the fish which still
run shadowy lines thru all that murk against the shifting bars of
shipping channel, slipping that traffic, that bottom:

'You sure find out
when you get all the rubbish from down there – lot of bark, papers,
bathroom papers – it's real messy sometimes. Trees & twigs &
branches, branches of trees even floating down there. & then there's,
I dunno what kind of plant it is, it's like a crabapple limb & it's
just full of little twigs, & that's a wicked one when it gets caught in
to a thin net. & ends of logs that have been cut, you know, stump
ends & round blocks drifting. The sawmills open their gates, you know
& let all their loose stuff out – when that comes dashing there's even
sawdust in the river.'

At bottom of this slippery time, it's her boat,
her feet on, managing the freshet, swollen, flooding (highest tides
of the year last week) water on water swell, with a wind running
norwesterly 'it gets pretty choppy here', 'I've been here with a blow
that's bin blowing 47 miles an hour – just big big waves washing
way up above the rocks.' 'See it's narrow & when the wind blows
those waves break & cross, it gets *real* rough.'

She runs in the
throat of time, voicing the very swifts & shallows of that river,
urging, in the dash of it, enough to keep up, to live on. When nets
are up 50%, fuel's up, & the packers taking chum salmon, undressed,
at 20 cents a pound, 'the same they sell in the stores dressed at $1.20,
while they're selling the roe they don't even pay us for at $2.20
a pound, clear profit' ...

Somehow they survive the oily waters swirling
under packers piling, bargeloads of herring sucked up, truckloads
left to rot, salmon on ice in the packerboats collecting twenty hours
a day,

Somehow they survive, this people, these fish,
survive the refuse bottom, filthy water, their choked lives,
in a singular dance of survival, each from each. At the
narrows, in the pressure of waves so checked & held by
'deep-sea frontage' it's the river's push against her, play of
elements her life comes rolling on, hair flying. In gumboots,
on deck with rubber apron ('it's no dance dress'), she'll take
all that river gives, willing only to stand her ground (rolling,
with it, right under her feet, her life, rolling, out from under,
right on out to sea ...

Response

'I think the fish like their water clean too,'
she says, with a dry laugh where: this outgoing
river, this incoming tide

                        mingle & meet. To take
no more than the requisite, *required* to grow, spawn,
catch, die: required to eat.

Intelligence (as if by radio?

                                    Moon river rising, raising a
ghost, Intensifies its run of living water (wind riffle
cold tonight) against this black, these mat pilings, solid as
deadheads, eaten away by time.

                              Light temporary (occasional cloud &,
she's moving west, as always, with our spin away from, knots of,
black chunks of history (old cannery pilings, old sheds rotting their
legs into the rapid run of water westward, to the sun's going,
to the open rising of the wind, easterly, betrays rain ... Full moon
one night in twenty-eight. Full moon minus rain one time in nine
of that, or thereabouts,

                        Night, I'm wanting to catch you *this* time
(the moon's unwinding burial blanket, time, stands in its warp
temporarily only, light –
                        Legs of, sheds, stumps, amputated limbs
(torn knots nets are, shadows only. Where's the *body* of this being
we run against? & feel, this net we're caught in, fish, light on
full, suddenly blinded in its extent:

This black & white we only half perceive is caught by a wave-
photography moon operates on a full night, quiet, most of the boats
out. Wave reading shed, telegraphy of pilings in the river's
intimate creak of hulls shatter – a dog bark somewhere, the sudden
chuckle of sea, someone scratching his head, turns in with the last
bilge into creeping water, splash. This continues ...

                                    & if the mono-
chrome of white & red, the sloping roofs of Canadian Fish resemble,
light in the moon like old siding Chinese backs rest beside, a pipe,
a break in the sun from soldering work – some cannery with its
clanking stream of cans, its steam, its rot of excessive fish
still on the dock of *that* time

if, behind the dyke (tracks),
there's a ghostly clutter of Indian tenement/Japanese cannery shacks
whose 'floor ... is littered with blankets, furniture, cooking tins,
fish gear, carnival masks, & usually 3 or 4 dogs' while 'over the
doorway is a board with L1356 or whatever happens to be the number
of the boat in which the man goes out to meet the salmon coming in'
and when 'a boat is found bottom up, its number is taken & the
inhabitants of that shack are notified'

& if there is still,
further along, under the gravel of cannery parking lot, a picket
fence, a woman's wailing all night long, for what? for what return
the present *doesn't* ride upon? It's not linear:

the stainless
steel lines going down in the Gulf echo other trollings, catch
in the mesh of a net we refuse to see, the accretion of all our
actions, how they interact, how they inter/read (intelligence),
receive, the reading the sea, a vanishing marsh, a dying river,
the mesh we are netted in, makes of *us.*

Life Cycle

after spawning they are exhausted, greatly
emaciated, & soon die, their bodies sinking
to the bed of the stream or lodging in the
drift at its side.

Flakes, flakes of fire, fish flakes. Or flaked out after the last
shift, flakey chips & salt grains on the tables of the Steveston,
beer going down cool & easy in the light, settling down into a
round chair, friends playing shuffleboard, chatting in the long
low hall, no wind.

                            Outside, flakes of moonlight on the
black river. Outside reeks of fish, like it always has. 'Today
we cook at Holly, Harlock & Wellington,' (1894). After the flood
'it's been a hard pull, but I think it's safe now with more
piling.'

       Safe against that river cresting at over 20 feet.
Safe again, forgetting she's a way in, to return, in time, the
stream. Against all odds they home in, to the source that's
marked their scales first birth place: environing:

                            It rings us
where we are (turn & turn about), however the depth   its cool
waters glide (over us), erase, with vast space elide the code
we've managed to forget: this urge to return, & returning, thresh,
in those shallows, death, leaving what slips by, the spore,
the spawn, the mark that carries on ... like a germ, like violence
in the flesh,

            as if, hooknosed, holding to the shape they burn in,
salmon don't re-enter time (in four years, the river), or,

In the long low hall where lights inexplicably darken & exhaust
their fire (& the canneries with long blackout drapes, the crepe,
the pall not elsewhere, over the Pacific, but here: 'you wouldn't
want to go outside ..'

as if the earth were dead
& we within it ash, eating ash, drinking the lead fire of our own
consumption, 'Here's to us!'

As if, 'outside,' a white fire *doesn't*
ring us, earth flicker its own circuits we, transparent, burn within.

Sun & Moon thru the Japanese Fishermen's Hospital (1898-1942)

Up the stairs; up the stairs, wild geese outside, wind blows thru your
hair, thru delta, marsh grass (up the stairs' silt, thick with it
hot with this *sun* that burns up off the sea / earth

                                        (hibiscus?

                                                        Up the
stairs it says Japanese Fishermen's Hospital, weathered, & the plank
siding, planks we climb up (the stairs: there is no way I can avoid
looking your look as you turn:

                                        wharf, boat, yard arms
& the moon glimmering its strange eye down river, down where the
mouth is.

            I've known you a long time, I've know you in this marshy
selvedge (thick with the rim of the earth's shadow turning, into sun.

            I've known this estuary light filled, Garry Light (its mouth
whose strands run wet with water sinking into white, barred, light.

            I've seen your hand on the weathered planking *this*
side of the hospital we climb, *against* the sun & into shadow, wait:
where blurred faces tranquil lie, afternoon sand across the wooden
floor, the nurse, this person dying or giving birth? a single red
hibiscus fading, into its glass.

We've come to where, what, changes at the heart: this General
Ward, white a, widow's mouth (sea glinting just offshore), a
mother's hole? We've come to generations, generation, Steveston,
at the heart: our death is gathering (salmon) just offshore, as,
back there in this ghostly place we have, somehow, entered (where?
you turn & rise, gently, into me.

Ghost,

oily ring shimmering, scintillating round the stern
of the boat you have just painted, *Elma K*, all your ties to shore,
your daughters, wife. Candy cache for the littlest grandchild
peering, short-frocked, over the pen where you, below water level,
fork up out of the deep – hooked, iced, dressed in slimey
death rendered visible – salmon.

'Nobody talks about them
anymore', the ghosts that used to rise when you, a child, crossing
the dyke from BC packers, night, saw, Out of the dark this strange
white light, or covering someone's rooftop, invisible to all but
strangers, this blue light telling of death.

(methane? invisible organic rot? We only know the extinction
of open marsh by concrete; the burial of burial ground by corporate
property.

But *then* there were places, you say, Chinaman's Hat,
where you couldn't sleep at night, fresh flower in your cabin, for
the host of restless souls' unburied hands outstetcht, returning,
claim their link with the decomposing earth

(ancestral: fertile as
death: hello briar rose, blackberry & trumpet flower. All their faces
lucent & warmlipt shining before your eyes: teachers, cabaret girls,
longlegged American army wives you chauffered, cared for, daughters,
friends of your daughters, down thru the water smiles of easy girls,
caught, kore, in the black hole of your eye, yourself a ghost now
of the natural world.

Were you fined? Did you cross the border inad-
vertently? Did chart & compass, all direction, fail? Interned,
your people confined to a small space where rebirth, will,
push you out thru the rings of material prosperity at war's
end fixed, finally, as citizens of an exploited earth:
you drive your own car, construct your own house, create your
registered place at Packers' camp, walk the fine (concrete)
line of private property.

But still, at night, tied up in some dark harbour,
it's the cries of women in orgasm you hear echoing, with the slap of
water against your hull, coming in, coming in, from far reaches
of the infinite world. And still, at sea, boundaries give way:
white women, white bellies of salmon thieved by powerful boats.

There are no territories. And the ghosts of landlocked camps are
all behind you. Only the blip of depth sounder & fish finder,
harmonic of bells warning a taut line, & the endless hand over
hand flip of the fish into silver pen – successive, infinite –

What do the charts say? Return, return. Return of what doesn't
die. Violence in mute form. Walking a fine line.

Only, always to dream of erotic ghosts of the flowering earth;
to return to a decomposed ground choked by refuse, profit, & the
concrete of private property; to find yourself disinherited from
your claim to the earth.

Or there is love

we'd house ourselves in, all this wind & rain.
Confuse us. Driving lines that shift, the floor does, ground or
under sea, to cast, at low tide what lies uncaught, uncovered
traces only, of sun & the moon's pull.

Unseen, how lines run
from place to place, How driving from town she follows the water's
push, the fields, drained by ditch to river to, the sea at,
where she lives ... 'At the end of the road,' she says
Steveston is. At the mouth, where the river runs under, in, to the
immanence of things.

To live in a place. Immanent. In
place. Yet to feel at sea. To come from elsewhere & then to discover
love, has a house & name. Has land. Is landed, under the swaying
trees which bend, so much in this wind like underwater weeds we think
self rises from.

But the place itself, mapt out, a web, was grass:
tall, bent grass swaying heavy with seed. Cottonwood whose
seeds make a web in the wind. 'It was a wild place – where foxes
might live,' this marsh persistent bending windswept lines of force,
current, men drag their nets thru to recover (as if they could)
wealth
(fishy as quick slime, saying, it's here, & here, & here,
this self
whose wealth consists of what?

A house? built by
hands & handed down from father to not son but daughter, tenuous as
moonlight sometimes, hair so strong sun weaves ladders in it, webs,
of strange connection. Light & dark. And so from this place to
center, dreaming of the source of things, flow, a ditch, from there to
... Japan & back? No, somehow love runs, shaken by the waters' pull
& leaves a network of men beached, Remembering now whose name,
in the dark the one owl calls & foxes' gloaming eyes, lit up by
the future (moon) say love, love will be ... a fisherman's dream,
the web, the snare ...

To retain, to remember, simply, the right names for things. Kneeling
by the bed, in a knotting of grass she seeks to see her life (oinari-san,
by the power of foxes) dreams: I found myself in a hall piled high with
dirty dishes, no one around, I had to wash them all. How they pile up,
these leftovers trapt, out of the flow. Like the fish. Like the
network of fishy familial parts these knots are, 'my daughter, my house',
these knots that bind.

                    At the end of the road, at the river's mouth,
muddy with all these empty dykes & misplaced hope, she's removed herself,
disappearing like foxes of the past into the underbrush, whose wall's
this briar hall of moonlight, whisper of old rituals: who are you now
you've cut yourself adrift, alone?
                                        'I'm not really in
the Japanese community, I don't belong to Buddhist Church, I don't
send my kids to sunday school.'

Who also, neither north or south, drives back, late, by the shining
watery roads from town, from the Western Front, from the center of things,
to mud & drainage ditch, familiar house, shit, the accumulation of
personal things. To the place of firstcomers where a woman felt
'like I was living in a wild field', where the grass, where the lines of
wind, where the lines of power moved clear in a field of power.

                              Where now her house stands
webbed with weaving, leaf tracery & light (of pots, plants), a house she
inhabits, immanent, at the edge of town a field they're raising houses on.
And coming from town, driving down by the scummy & soontobecovered ditches
(remnant, of leftover rains, plucked cabbages in the sun, & wind) where do you
find her, out?
              as now by day,
                            or in, summer's wilder growth, around &
past (the stepping stones at back are wood & cut by hand) amidst (there is
no closer) hands full of beans & fingers in the heart of, 'well I *live* here',
lettuce, children, friends, you find a self, under the trees that sway like
underwater weeds, connecting things.

Steveston, BC

Steveston: delta, mouth of the Fraser where the river empties, sandbank after
sandbank, into a muddy Gulf.

Steveston: onetime cannery boomtown: 'salmon capital of the world': fortunes
made & lost on the homing instinct of salmon.

Steveston: home to 2,000 Japanese, 'slaves of the company': stript of all their
belongings, sent to camps in the interior away from the sea, wartime, who
gradually drift back in the '40's, a few who even buy back their old homes,
at inflated prices, now owning modern ranchstyle etc, & their wives,
working the cannery, have seniority now, located.

Steveston: hometown still for some, a story: of belonging (or is it continuing?
lost, over & over …

                                       Steveston divided into lots with an ox
barbecue, sold the lot but only bit by bit Steveston belongs to its temporal
landowners & those who, Packers & Nelson Brothers, Canadian Fish, hold chunks of
the waterfront like gaps (teeth) of private territory, 'use at your own risk,'
but the shark (with his teeth dear) speculates, brooding on housing developments
whose sidewalks pave over the dyke, whose street lamps obliterate the shadow
bowl of night on Lum Poy's field, west, & south, as the geese fly past the old
Steves place & on, to dark to
                              wherever fish come from, circling back in
to their source:

                   We obscure it with what we pour on these waters, fuel, paint, fill,
the feeding line linking us to Japan & back, wherever, cargo ships, freighters
steam up river & only the backwaters house these small boats whose owners,
displaced & now relocated as fishermen can be, fishing up nets full of shadow/
food for the canneries to pack, blip blip sonar & even these underwater
migrations visible now as routes, roots, the river roots, out from under

                                                           brail net
they lift these fishes with, reading a river gulf, Or, visibly

how it pours, this river, right over the top of the rock damn into Cannery Channel
swirling freshet on & right on past the sedge that roots sediment, witness these
gaptoothed monument pilings, pile stumps of ghostly canneries settle, into
obscurity (a map necessary, or key, to the old locations) locating thus
(where are we?) shipwreck, a rusty wheel, a drum, inarticulate emblems of
this life craft that runs, that continues, this busy work of upkeep (*without*
us) wheeling its river bank into sun, into the blind anonymity of sea light,
the open
        sun. a sea men sink their lives into, continue, dazzlingly undeciphered,
unread days, dazed with the simple continuance of water pour, of wind, of small
stores turning their annual credit ledgers, debit, silent as winter falls, falls,
pours.

                This is the story of a town, these are the people, whose
history locates inside of dream, in site of (in situ) down by the riverbank a
torrent pouring past its sloughs & back channels, boat basins time repeats, this
one was Phoenix, this one Atlas, or leaving Hong Wong/Wo's obliterated letters,
even whole names along with bits of crockery water washes, dead dogs, web caught
up under the shadows of these buildings men would cast, like nets of retrieval,
only to cast their names across the line that water washes, away, incessant,
swollen, by reaches of the sea our lives respond to, irresistibly drawn, these
precarious floats, boats equipt with the latest machinery, radar, sonic scan,
drifting, limbs extended, sometimes logs & deadheads, sometime creatures of
motive that swim, *against* the source, but always continuing to return, always
these lovely & perilous bodies drifting in spawn, swarm on out to sea.

Notes

'Not to be Taken': quoted material from the Richmond Art
Center's oral history files – interviews with William Gilmore and
Les Gilmore.

'A by-channel; a small backwater:' with thanks, Inez Huovinen.

'Intelligence': quoted material from 'Steveston-by-the-Fraser',
Garnett Weston, *British Columbia Magazine*, August 1911.

'Life Cycle': paragraph quoted from Dr. J.P. Babcock's treatise
on Pacific salmon in Appendix 3 of Cicely Lyons' book,
Salmon: Our Heritage, B.C. Packers Ltd., 1969. Other
material in this poem quoted from the same book.

Don McKay
Long Sault

I So Long

See

the new islands
submerged highways
man-made cut
parkway
control dam
Eisenhower lock
Barnhart Island park site
Saunders Moses Power Dam
dikes.
Ride over the once famous Long Sault Rapids.
Boat leaving every 2 hours — 9 AM to 7 PM.

Dam

Into the dam
the river has been wound
the way God reckons up the souls of men
and tots the till.

Not coiled, curled.
The new lake does not strain or brim
behind the dam.
It sleeps.
It nuzzles the muddy shore as a vacuum cleaner
purrs across the carpet.

Bedrock

We were ready for extravagance
that day, on the bottom
of the river where the Long Sault
used to be
                        In the park the inmates
                        their sunken eyes in the grey
                        grey flesh
                                    they wear
                        an awkwardness, move
                        as guests in nature, thinking
                        not gotterdammerung not
                        stomp that pulp but
                        whitewall   whitewall   whitewall
It was the dullness
embarrassed us, cover it up we
thought, being merely interested
in the rock that pestled its kettle for centuries
in the slab aslant you can feel
the absent turbulence.
An empty gym.

The slide shows us lying, 3 kids
on a slab on one of those faceless
washed-out days that never peaks
or makes a story of itself.
I am wearing my basketball jacket.
And what there is/
           is old, older
than ear, older than nose.
What is salience to this
power of roundness that surrounds
those kids,
their adolescent pyramids?
Rubble. Be ground. Children, there are
no accidents (or is it
only accidents? I can't
remember).

It is a tale full of its endings.
There are all these poems standing
like plumbers amid the ruined buildings
gesturing tool boxes
at the absence of bathrooms in the air, is this
some sort of a joke?
And only the Long Sault is laughing:
Fuck your renaissance, get me a beer.

At the Long Sault Parkway

The noise, the continual motion, and magnitude
of the contending waves, render the Longue
Sault, at once an object of terror and delight;
these burst upon each other, and tossing aloft
their broken spray, cover the stream with a white
and troubled surface, as far as the eye can extend.

And now you're nostalgia, you're a bowl of mushroom soup
tepid and tumid,
teeming with fat carp who feed on your reedy bottom.
But everything's so tasteful, isn't it, so
nice, really, the way they fixed things up with beaches and
everything, and the picnic areas.
No sutures, no Frankenstein bolts through the neck, only
the dam at the end of the lake, a white wink
like a distant TV set
betrays the operation.

You're better off now, rocking on the porch, you lap
lap, lap at the shores of memory,
counting to infinity by ones.
You have old chums here.
These islands are the tops of hills
you used to lash and gnaw.
And here's old Highway 2 who followed you
everywhere.
Always the comic, now he surfaces
to hump an islet
and subside.

I have to go. Rest easy
and so long.

Will your anchor hold in the storms of life?

Christ Church (c. 1837) owes its existence to the
munificence of Adam Dixson, U.E., reputed to be
the first man to have harnessed the water power
of the St. Lawrence.

Seen through these panes of antique glass
everything undulates, breathes
as a pump organ.
My fellow tourists deepen
like tourists in a poem or a goldfish bowl.

Yet the church is simple
and straightforward as a hymn.
Without the sign or the brochure I recognize
the church that used to snag the mind
of Moulinette, that
relocated village

> Here lies
> Christ Church
> Moulinette
> relocated
> Neither dead
> nor alive
> but suitably
> commemorated.

The shell is haunted by a wordless music now.
A susurration flows through the pews
and browses past the altar, nine to five,
observing the classical mouldings and gothic windows
with their antique imperfect panes.
It is architecture, it is history, there
is nothing to lament/ unless
the one who heaves with a grunt a dirt brown burlap sack
to the back of his rusting chevy pickup once
in Moulinette.

A feeling of if, a feeling of but, a field of fire hydrants

For a time, we were
amazement —
        they got
        this house-moving machine with tires so big I can
        show you the picture my brother standing up
        inside the hub he is ten years old that can move
        a house so gentle they just leave the pictures on the walls —

unfettered, soaring in suspension of feeling

The rhetoric was
a shepherd to us (though later
we might have said superintendent without sensing
any change) the way
we could be inside its shell but never
really know which history
was being made, and never asking
whose.

Here was a map coming out in dotted lines
to be filled in with the right answer.
Here was a rapids in the noose.
Here was a field of fire hydrants waiting for a town.
Here was a marina in the field of fire hydrants
waiting for the water to arrive
to whisper sibilant up to the waiting wharf.

The river was about to swell.
It was doing the Charles Atlas course, would be
the servile giant.
Its language was unlocked: Power & Prosperity,
                              Development & Growth
Look at that bicep
                    (or that
snake-bit arm we would never completely think,
or think only as far as
the feeling of if
the feeling of but, never to the fettering flag-
planting noun, as though
the making of the feeling and
the making of the dam were cognate
pregnancies
              (or carbuncles, as we
couldn't have said until we'd seen, a feeling
of if, a feeling of but, a feeling of smelling,
even when we named our humdrum town
'City of Power and Progress', smelling
its industries still smoking at both ends like cigars.

II Reading a Rapids

Reading a rapids on the Gens de Terre

Whether to shoot or portage, whether
to ride the thin shell through
or turtle it around?
I stood on a rock and watched her
and the roar
was weather
a big soft push.
    Don't stand on the verandah boy,
    step inside
    and I'll spread my peacock's tail of gurgles and cackles, purls
    and groans.
    I'm a Berlitz school of languages, monsieur
    I'm a stew.
    I'm the glue that holds it all together, son
    I'm the AEIOU
    and sometimes Y,
    I'm the answer to your Hebrew alphabet.
    I'm a multitude murmuring its beads
    in Mecca, in Moscow, in St. Peter's Square.
    Slide down my throat boy, I'm a feast
    of flickering tongues and curls
    lascivious as Beardsley, sweet as Shirley Temple,
    chastely my sealsmooth buttocks drape the bones
    below.
    Cher lonesome voyageur, come in
    and I'll come into you.

She gets too intimate, too fast.
Her voice reads you like braille while you read her
plotting her traps, her unsuspected teeth.
Too bad, I said out loud, we'd never make it in one piece.
She'd catch us broadside as we tried to sweep
around that bastard of a rock,
swamp the canoe and bash us good.

Across the portage the voice pursues us still
biting into spirit as the thwart bites into flesh.
Someday — I always add this —
I'll go back.

Wolflip

It hangs a rim
on our reality:
                    here is an edge
wolflip
the first curl of the rapids, smile
that sheathes the teeth.
It waits, or rather
it disdains to wait, stillstanding, still
smiling, a wave that will not break
or ebb or mime the motions of the heart
like the stories told by waves that break on a beach.

Wolflip
that mona lisa snarl
troubles the blood
seizes on the body of the hypnotized canoe.
We must be swallowed but
we must be swallowed whole –
                    the thought
honed on the current like a sharp
is gathered in the wrist, to paddle with the flow
and yet resist,
to sing obliquely through
                    we slip
swiftly as bleeding to the edge, good-bye, good-bye, and
where is Jacques and where is Virginie and hang
upon the inbreath, on the ache to
plunge
plunge down the throat that leaps to meet you now, the thundering
          and when I throw open the door hey the stillness
          is shouting she turns from the stove a stray wisp dangling
          on her cheek you horses ass she says the wind
          beating against us in the thundering
applause.

The Great Blue Heron

What I remember
about the Great Blue Heron that rose
like its name over the marsh
is touching and holding that small
manyveined
wrist
upon the gunwale, to signal silently —
                                        look

The Great Blue Heron
(the birdboned wrist).

— deer

and came that morning down the dusty road
into the deer's
virginity —
                gone, white flag flashed
did you see it flashed
like a
like a fridge left crisp & clean in the mind
all day

The Great Canadian Short Story

She chops wood
she chops wood
on the campsite in Jasper in
Riding Mountain she
chops, the chips
fall where they may
in Pancake Bay in Manitoulin
she chops and the logs (the soap-
fleshed prairie poplar aromatic
BC cedar whunk reliable pine the
woodchoppers Holiday Inn cachunk) part
like a curtain, drop, pleased, a kid
taking a bow for this
the inside story of our trip she
chops and
burns.

III Last Laughs

The River is Laughing to Itself

When Sally is dancing, first
her left foot, now

her body's wriggling into old time tunes
bowed, sewn on the fiddle, breaking
down, become

becoming's what we're ravelling
and Joe and I ka-
chunk kachunk are keeping time

are keeping time suspended as a tent
taut and entranced as we

dance and are
dancing when Sally is.

Off the Road

The road's still busy in the blood
when we pitch camp and cook
and eat our Irish stew.
Pine smoke drifts slowly through cracks in the traffic.

The kids float sticks
down the creek behind the campsite
while we sip our coffee by the fire.
The moon
hangs over the tent like a neutral traffic light that leaves us
uhh just about to say something that
we don't

Dusk is almost better than a word.

A kingfisher chatters from the shore.
A tickertape
in an empty office talks to itself.

It's time to go for a paddle, time to weave us
into the intricate quietnesses just
to quit our listening & hear & trail
your fingers in the water the kingfisher
chattering WHITE-TAILED DEER AWARDED SENATE POST &
dives & snatches silver wriggling from the bay & let
the motion you can never tell Joe says what will
happen when you paddle the canoe the motion be
your motion till you look up at the stars and ask
why not? the kingfisher
chattering, since time
began the 401 has been flogging its dong all the way to Toronto.

Along about then

Along about then this new mountie, Macmillan,
Macdonald, something like that come down here
sayin how he's going to clean up all the stills,
and they was plenty, in the township.
>   The others grinning already, they've
>   heard it from uncles or grandfathers
>   in kitchens scrubbed like this one with a Scots
>   ferocity, so clean, another thing we always said,
>   that you could get right down there on your hands
>   and knees and eat right off the floor, so clean
>   linoleum spits the sunlight fft a cat's hiss
>   at the white enamel pot that's sitting on the stove
>   which ffts it off again
Nope. Tromped her up and down and couldn't find a thing. Remember
mowin with my father in the front field here come Macmillan,
yes I believe he was a Macmillan, and maybe four five men
draggin themselves out of Kennedy's bush just up the road.
Looks like they been fightin bears in there.
Figured they'd come right through the swamp because some joker
told them Kennedy was making hooch.
Course he never touched the stuff.
So
here they come past us down the road, lookin
normal as they could covered in mud, and Pa
just holds out his jug and offers them a swig.
Pa said afterwards
Macmillan must've figured we was drinkin corn the way
he stared, his jaw grindin and
just marched on past us down the road.
Course all it ever was was only lemonade.
>   We all chuckle.
>   The kitchen, the afternoon, the beer bottles
>   catching a little sun inside themselves, the pause
>   is full of stories waiting to be told.

Nope. Never found a thing and even when
they busted up that still of old Lalonde's it wasn't
any mountie found out where it was.
They say the game warden's ridin down the branch
near old Lalonde's place when he come acrost this deer just
standin there beside the road starin at him.
So
he gets out of his wagon thinkin this's strange, he
walks up to the deer still standin there
and pushed it over with his hand.
Like that.
Drunk as a skunk.
                    Well
maybe the skunks *was* drunk cause it appeared
that old Lalonde and his boys been getting lazy and just
tossed their mash across the fence.
Probably polluted half the game in the township
before they caught him.

    The chuckle's more a rumble deep down. Everybody
    has a sip of beer.
    Now the story
    will be mulled and tinkered with a rickety
    contraption made of names
                names
                names like the roads
    they cut and stumped and walked and
    rode reach back to other Kennedys
                    Lalondes
                      Macmillans men
    who could walk to Montreal and carry back
    a hundred pounds of seed, along
    about then, conjured in that kitchen sun.

Paddling in November

Not on but in,
to.
No leaf drifts to the black
surface of the stream it
acts, and catquick.
                    Every
stroke we bite is deep and crisp and rich
in protein we unzip
the water cleanly, honing,
parting
the banks we enter and
we enter still
thirsting after, cleaving
to the thrum the other
music
utterly (ambush)
drinks.

The Long Sault Life Insurance Company

Even on the homebound bus
matter and energy may be one
exquisite form.

At this point the poem is dreaming of fiddles, of fingers
dancing upon fiddles, of dancing
managing the fingers dancing on the fiddles, of a woman
brushing her teeth.
                                        I wake
upon the pavement, holding door open
while alighting.   A tree.
Very well, a tree beside a car, reaching over
the car.   A man.
A man fixing his car beneath a tree: memoranda.
But from whom, to whom
are they addressed
etcetera.
This goes on and on, verandah
after verandah down the block
until, like the period
My House Sits
smug, smug as a mother, fits
snugger than rhyme and yet
alembic,
its what you most expect that sometimes
catches you awares
and cooks your casserole, tunes your fiddle and other
tropes: tricks.

Inside, the kids
begin a game in which my entry
(The Monster is coming! Hide!
Hide under the sofa!)
is anticipated.

The River is Laughing to Itself (continued)

Trying to make the jump to the Capitachouane
we followed this creek that
twisted and
giggled itself silly, haha very funny, going
shallow & one damn beaver dam after another of the sons of
over we go & finally we figured
this heres a fallopian tube going nowheres & somebody
says nope this heres the ghost of the
pecker of the last guy tried to make the jump
to the Capitachouane
                        and now
years as they say later leaning
over the rapids for one moment
I get caught for one moment, I get
occupied, though just
for a moment by the dance that
unmoves movers and the
urgency of blood becomes ah but there
I poise when
in
falls my papermate
ballpoint
pen.

IV The ghost with a hammer

Long Sault Blues

Well I don't know where that Long Sault's got to
It's just dry bone all the time
Yes I don't know where that Long Sault's got to
And it's dull as that dry bone bottom all the time
And I'm waiting here with his unemployment cheque Charlie
For that long gone Long Sault man of mine.

Well they took me down to the river
And they showed me a heap of bones
Yes they took me down to the dried up river
And they showed me these bald old stones
Said that is all he ever was goodbye forget him
You're better off just living on your own.

So I'm standing by the highway
With my suitcase by my side
Yes I'm standing on the 401 highway
And I'm thinking suicide
And I don't care where you're going to mister
Cause there's something here that's died.

But then I heard he was up north in Kapuskasing
With his big gold saxophone
Yes I heard he was in a bar in Kapuskasing
Making that same old sort of chucklin moan
And yes they said that he was chasing
Every piece of tail around for sale or loan.

Well when I heard that powerful news
I just broke down and cried
And when I moaned and sung the blues
It lit my fire inside
Now I'm going to find that Long Sault man
No matter where he hides.

And when I catch that man again
I'm going to fetch my crock of dandelion wine
Yes when that son of a bitch shows up again
We're going to sit and drink that 15 gallon crock of dandelion wine
Cause there's moves that he knows Charlie
You just can't buy in the five and dime.

The Long Sault Rapids in Kapuskasing

I guess you could say there was time
about him
though it wasn't any worn down suit or shoes.
Maybe the way he'd say
it doesn't signify a fart
when people asked him what he meant.
Folks figured he was wise
he told me, because he never said a thing they could understand.
And he blew a smoke ring through a smoke ring, punctuating,
maybe.

I'll buy a beer I says
before you play again.
A beer, he says, is worth the truth.
We mourn
here but we never know what for.
Now you – tilting his glass in my direction – you
suck up to life.
You're hoping one day she'll come across, the Halifax whore
done up like a regular virgin bride.
But you know she won't. Know why?
I shook my head.
She ain't.

I think this over (ain't *what?*)
while he plays
his big gold saxophone not to
but underneath the buzzing of the bar.
Blue Moon, Night Train
I can't give you anything but love.
It isn't mournful and it isn't real unhappy
but melancholy as blood thinking about itself.

One other thing, he says on his way to the mens,
you better write this down.
A saxophone ain't worth a damn.
But it ain't a dam, neither.

I never thought to ask him
what the spelling of it was.
but I know what he'd say.

The ghost with a hammer

Well the big news from the world of sport tonight
is the challenge bout between Maalox and the Long Sault Rapids.
After the first five seconds during which Maalox threw
just about every punch in the book it was
strictly no contest, folks, and the plucky colloid had to be helped
from the ring suffering from excess gas, acid
and stomach discomfort.
The Long Sault was, as usual, gracious in victory.
'The kid's got guts' he told reporters in his dressing room,
'but he reads like an insurance agent!'
Right after the fight he left with his sparring partner the poetry of
Margaret Avison
for a holiday at an unspecified location.

The Long Sault Dada Liberation Front

It's by the lens-splintered sun flick flick flick
between the evergreens we know
we are moving through the Great Canadian North, winging
on that high thin chord held by the violin while
flick the trees diminish flick the white
comes forward at us until
                    clannnnnnnnnnnnnnnnnnng
the Arctic edge that rolls away and sucks
your eyes out, lifting slightly now the screen
just wiped in white and right across
where the horizon ought to be appears
in those penultimate letters The National Film Board of Canada
Presents, the clang,
swelling, growing pregnant with its Here It Comes Folks and about
to burst in melody, when
                    whunk.
A terribly small soft body being dropped.
O Jesus,
we're in black and white.
We fade in slowly on the Long Sault Rapids in an old trenchcoat
smoking. Nondescript surroundings.
He gets up slowly from the bench.
Slowly he unbuttons the trenchcoat.
He looks like a slightly gone wrong Spencer Tracy
benign and smiling.
He unbuttons his fly.
He pulls out a sign.
The sign says
'And now, back to the show.'

The Long Sault Rapids' Grandmother

The Characters:

Trees lisping whispering
Grandma rocking knitting
Bald Cat stretching scratching
Long Sault smoking joking to himself
The Telephone
just sitting there

The Action:

knit
knitknit
knititit
the Long Sault Rapids' Grandma's needles flashing thru
the pant suit she is knitting for the cat
out of the fur he's shed,
her rockers going waste not
                          want not
                  waste not
                          want not
                                      o
she really knew a thing or two.

The Long Sault
smoking at her, dumb old shit
naked came Old Baldy into the world and hence – a slow
o smokes across the porch and
frays and lisps off in the trees –
he shall dismiss, sans teeth
sans eyes, sans knitted
metafur.

So smokes
the witty bard, the rockers meanwhile
                    waste not
                          want not
and the grandma
knitititing sharply in reply, the bald cat
scratching, telephone
still sitting there.

Round two, the Long Sault smokes,
the telephone.
It sits there and it never rings a note.
Why you
can rock your way around the world and wind up
talking to yourself.
So much – he hangs this smoke ring in the air –
for metafurs.

Now grandma stops her rocking, puts
her knitting down for the first time since
o time out of mind
and looks her smartass grandson in the eye.
That telephone, she snaps, is just
a conversation piece.
Reckon I always like the way
it cradles its receiver on my table there, but son –
she picks it up –
it ain't attached.

It isn't.
The Long Sault sucks
astonishment into a jaded lung.
The trees, the bald cat, and the telephone
hang on the inhalation till he coughs.
Goddam, he says at last, the absence of a wire
whangs there like a goddam tambourine.
That's better son, she rocks, you just
keep on knitting them like that.

This was maybe the first dumbfounding and last horse laugh
the Long Sault ever suffered through.

Long Sault Breakdown

hotcha
what's that purling at the edge of thinking its
                    hotcha Mille Roches
                    hey there Moulinette

LONG SAULT

looking for an opening
sniffing like a wolverine
                    Morrisburg
                    Iroquois
ready for your entry now

LONG SAULT

looking for a body he can seize and dance through
twitching at the skirts of the lady at the bus stop
hanging in the talking in the all night restaurant

LONG SAULT

here comes the Rapids Prince
steaming down the river with
                    raftsman
                    Indian
                    coureur de bois come
hop on board for the resurrection run through

LONG SAULT

aggravating
activating
hey that moonlight flicker those tongues those curls that
Chute you bastards down the silvery v gotta
dig that paddle gotta here comes another now
Sweep
                    c'mon
                    c'mon
                    c'mon

LONG SAULT

        log float
        busted boat
here come the voyageurs drowned and dancing
glistening bones in the old soiree and
hotcha
the drunk who was swept clean through its
        a miracle
              a joker
       a juggler
            a fiddler
       a gargler
a metaphysician drinking dandelion wine that's
                     LONG SAULT

you can
lock him up constable
shut him out citizen
he'll drink your liquor and he'll steal your woman, hey
catch that motherfucker never letcha pants down
c'mon now kiddies while I spin you a tale
about the thunder and the blood
and the virgin and the purleyman choose
your partners for the
                     LONG SAULT

Robin Blaser
The Moth Poem

A Literalist

the root and mirror
of a plant
             its shape
and power familiar
iris

the light is disturbed by
the boxwood   leaves
shining
             rosemary
green, unblossoming
(the earth is too damp)

the eye catches
almost a tune

the moth in the piano
wherein
             unhammered
the air rings with

an earlier un
ease of the senses
disturbed (by Mrs. Arpan,
wife of a sailor

The Literalist

the wind does not move on
to another place

bends into,
as in a mirror,
                    the
breaking

the moth in the piano
will play on
frightened wings brush
the wired interior
of that machine

I said, 'master'

Between

the morning face of
turns you who
turn

      a complete
interior furniture
flecked with
the children
of the moth
          how
loud you are
against glass

the strings of / play on

this
     that
          now scattered

The Borrower

the one loved is
holding a moth
thin, metallic dark
model with a triangular
crest

what's out and secret
spills
the wind dries
moves on

                the interior
of his body
                   red water
with white threads
                      the bone
a ghost of his thigh
                   pale
blue gut holding the shit

highway

Awake

in the dark morning you are circled
by loss of sleep   you lean forward
from the balcony to see the moth
dying in the window   swept by
still wings

loose pieces of air fall
cold and catch your eyelids

the words don't fit you

your back is a mirror   your
hand a bowl holding the musical
moth

Supper Guest

leaning over the white
linen which casts

a pale light
over his face,

we are not deprived
the white bowl

must shine
behind our words,

leave us
in a fire of clouds

the tin flowers
the castles

which drift out
of our mouths

whitely
in the cold air,

fantômes
de sentiments

magic juices
on the eyelids,

so it is
what is met

a white moth carries its moth-body
trying the way into corners

The Medium

it is essentially reluctance   the language
a darkness, a friendship, tying to the real
but it is unreal

the clarity desired, a wish for true sight,
all tangling

'you' tried me, tried the everyday which
caught me, turning the house

in the wind, a lovecraft   the political
was not my business   I could not look

without seeing the decay, the shit poured
on most things, by indifference, the personal

power which is simply that,   demanding a friend
take dullness out of the world   (he doesn't know
his lousy emptiness)   I slept
in a fire   on my book bag, one dried wing

of a white moth   the story is of a man
who lost his way in the holy wood

because the way had never been taken without
at least two friends, one on each side,

and I believe my dream said one of the others
always led   now left to acknowledge,

he can't breathe, the darkness bled
the white wing,   one   of the body

of the moth that moved him, of the other
wing,   the language is bereft

O-friend

it was time you came
this night   you were NO

man attached to his opposite,
seen through a gate   or handed

his hat   you were as held
in a vase   orange calendula

and hot pink geraniums in blue
glass   that tropism

made you laugh   and the room,
is it possible you do not exist

separate from that glow
when I turned the flashlight

on the door?   who is there
who came dragging his

bag of tears? and remained
invisible   the whine is

not in me   is not part
of the moth who escapes

the cold in my electric
blanket   I suppose

I heard the dark and
with the craft wrought

against memory, it should
have been of no consequence

but the bones breathe, that
frame of what is contained,

opposites   the Sorrows sit
nearby surely,   cracking

their paws   once,the I
came on the Lady Bugs' home

at the foot of a redwood
they swarmed in heaps

their shells and loosened wings
flew in the wind of my steps

and once, Proteus, the goldfish,
jumped out of his bowl,   left

the color of dried orange peel
and so it is a turn of the wheel

you left   a kind of music,
la-de-da   and stink

in the air   held close
with the invisible rose,

O-*imaginarie-in-knowledge*

Invisible Pencil,

one does not willingly take the honey
sweet plant,   the words are lost, the
holy language simultaneous with this speech,

and flatteries, this participation in mirrors,
turns from the streets of some minds
one follows another man who kissed his shadow

now a moth flies overhead to the floorlamp,
stops my reading the *Death of Virgil,*
form fixed and mute,   one element

participates in his travels
more than another, watery source
as if the hometown river flowed

into the room and out of the heart

Atlantis

draws back from the shine on the water,
the crumbling pieces flow unattached

the cement patches, the fit of the dark
streets around the towers   the wet

touches   spring a trap in personal
history,   interior, riotous   smokers

of poetry bathe among the ruins,
slip off the rocks,   green and

waking with weeds of the sea
the technical movement is made

by the water harp   in *moth-time*
the waves lift the bunched-up

newspaper, full of foam,   then
looking up, I see it run back, *defecate*

to a pure transparency,   the castles,
the lighted cliffs

Atlantis

the light of it, as he felt himself perish,
the *riotous moth,*   back and forth

there is a spilled glass of water, an ocean
spreading on the table

under the shine on the water, the pieces
flow, unattached   it will be that

horseplay the mouth takes for milk,   the
fit of the rivers around the books,

ashtrays, yellow apple and pomegranate
here   the web falls, sticky,   holding

the forehead   the apparent violence
bathed in,   a key to this privacy

he leaned over his poem   a piece
of blood fell out of his head   dazzling

clock sounds, the riotous moth, happiness
and this habit of light   *the sad soul*

wanders about *a spirit like an image*
this image enters the ghost
                    ly sent iment

My Dear ⸺⸺

> we end with you
circling your garden, allowing
the officials to lead you in,
trivial and cheap at Gump's,
the worthless mention of Snellgrove,
Pomeroy, Hack divided, phony last
suppers, démodé drips on the California
landscape, fake spooks in the upper
right hand corner of the orange machine,
brief agony for the dining room wall
at a price,   you,coming to
ignore this language

which is colored, takes in slime, is
some center where one is helpless
even to oneself,   flowers of the mouth,
it is smoke, alive only in the
car lights,   is stationary,

considered as paint full of secrets   flows,
still on the wall like a moth   until
it is pushed, then separating

with an outward stammer, officially
immortal,   to feed itself,   the final
thing
>   somebody else's idea

Paradise Quotations

the stairs did not creak, but the snow did
I fixed the telescope and looking through I saw
a stag
        on the way back I saw the traces
of blood, but no longer believed in their
existence

first in translucent lymph with cobweb-threads
the Brain's fine floating tissue swells, and spreads

the marble hand, probably from its contact
with the uncharmed harp, had strength to
relax its hold and yield the harp to me

nerve after nerve the glistening spine descends
the red Heart dances, the Aorta bends

the white rose of Eddy-foam, where the stream
ran into a scooped or scalloped hollow of the
Rock in its channel   this Shape, an exact
white rose, was for ever overpowered by the
Stream rushing down in upon it, and still
obstinate in resurrection it spread up into
the Scallop, by fits and starts, blossoming
in a moment into a full Flower

through each new gland the purple current glides,
new Veins meandering drink the refluent tides

for here would be the moonbeams on the ice,
glittering through a warrior's breastplate
        whenever a breeze went by, it swept the old
men's heads, the women's beauty, and all the
unreal throng, into one indistinguishable
cloud   ever-anxious crowd

edge over edge expands the hardening scale,
and sheathes his slimy skin in silver mail

it   it   it   it

a white shadow there on the glass,
the white T-shirt   turns that

are no longer an end
less meaning   leans forward to the

shaping, to find it, a flutter of the
darkness, but it ducks back

from the open slit of the window,
a cinnamon moth enters
and amorous, the lamp takes
it   came from the back

garden planted with pale flowers
that might show in the dark   it
mocked, tripped, then toted its
image, having no past, unprepared

the *moth-kiss* has two languages,
the one everyday, dusty, habitual,
and part delight, the other
an *unexpended myth* washes against

the glass, to be abstract, untied
by the friendship, the moment caught

Salut

you, priest, must know why you strike
tearing, teasing in that silly personality
if you fell, it is the rain falling down
the hanging pot of ivy, each leaf a-light
the grass of my eyes holding to a point,
the dew,   the spring

the piano, it was a gift, a promise of a debt
of music   it was a moth under the strings,
frantic to escape, played
   wings eyed like an owl came to the lamp

the cold has come, the moths have gone,
white, grey, cinnamon and one rested
in the sun, wine purple wings, yellow
edged, tacked with the wind's changes,
careened, then, taking flight, hid
in the fig tree

the circles   the moon, the stars, the
plants and below, under the earth, the sun
between the earth and the moon, a tone
beyond that, the lyre

asleep, the four oval paintings, stories alive,
the artist of the moth, his foot upon the lion's
paw of the table   there is no storm in the
glass, only the white edge of a sleeve, the
form, nothing beyond that I   I

further asleep, there are petunias, white, red,
rose and night, zinnias, red, violet, orange, roses,
silver and yellow, nasturiums, yellow, pansies, blue,
hollyhocks, pastel and waxy, violets, lilacs, sumac,
castor-bean flowers, flags, purple, white, brown

what is the day,   what is the charm, she, her
madness, yours, musical poplars, the mind
nearly destroyed by the presences, the fine
points which have no beginning

restless jewels   she is from the-light on the rails,
a-light running miles to a point   she is
in the house, an old railroad coach placed
on foundations by the railbed   among golden rod
and hop vines   she stands in the middle
of the room with arms outstretched, to protect
the bat, which caught, brown and velvet, she
puts to her breast against the yellow apron

this flower which is no flower   this new
land   the day filled with invisible princes,
Dr. Dolittle, the moon, the flow of rain
lighting the ivy   there is no meaning here,
there is all meaning here   Fran and Stan
laughing, the blue glass is $9.oo, the Houssin
Isadora Duncan, looking more like Rodin's Balzac
is $350   there is nothing here but an intense,
interior monologue with moments of color, forms
flowing toward beloved plants   the cost has
been high   when all the world is loved by the
daimon of mediocrity,   you, priest,

must know why you strike

C
D
♭E
G
A
♭B
B
D

The Translator: A Tale

first, the pool of water   just waking my arms hold
it   the circle of the cold morning air

last night's coffee spoon sticks to the drainboard
under it the clear print of a brown moth, made of sugar,
cream, coffee with chicory, and a Mexican spoon of blue
and white enamel

The ashtray is full and should be emptied before working that translation,   *Attis ran to the wooded pastures*
of the weavers of gold, the shadowy place, where as if a
bee stung his brain, he took a flint knife and let the
weight of his cock and balls drop from him,   so

when she felt her limbs lose her manhood, still with
fresh blood spotting the ground, she grabbed the drum
with snowy hands, beating the polished hide with soft
fingers, she rose to sing to her companions

the mound of cigarette buts moves, the ashes shift,
fall back on themselves like sand, startle   out of
the ashes, awakened by my burning cigarette, a brown
moth noses its way,   takes flight

Frank Davey
King of Swords

i   The death of Arthur continues.
When I bought her black peignoirs
he was dying, when I wrote her aubades
he was dying, when I took ill at her refusal
his fever rose with mine, his bile
convulsed, upward.

ii   The king of swords, standing
at the doorway of kingdom.
Does he desire
all that we've desired? –
warmth, the tearing of flesh,
the cries of babes? God
help him, all these ephemera,
swords in stone, scabbards,
butterflies.

iii   Don't
take it! That sword
has stabd the rock
you are, I am,
Mr Arthur. What an emblem
of rule: incest, fratricide,
a barren wife,
a bastard king.

iv   All the time we were married
I removed
kitchen knives from where she had hid them
on the table or counter, hid them
in drawers, fearing
their blade in my hand
her blood on the blade
& me, over her, completing
her dream, her king
of swords.

v   The battle at Bedegraine – all
         those young boys – Sir Griflet,
         King Clariaunce, Sir Kay,
         Gwimiart de Bloi –
         cock-proud, cunt-blinded.

         If only they had killd him,
         their king – instead
         driving their lances
         into the bowels of horses,
         sparring with broken beerbottles,
         switch-blades – letting
         their blood to embroider
         royal flags, ladies' bosoms,
         Modern Romances.

vi   Your hand
         nearing the hilt
         the double edges, the sundered
         stone.

         Wanting you to lead
         pavillions, trumpets, colord
         armour. You,
         carbon-base man.

vii   So early the steel
       shines to entrance us.
       & I only a child
       across the road from home
       watching the bulldozer
       back, & rear again, again
       into the fir & sapling maples
       while birds
       gorged themselves beneath the blade
       on worms.

viii   Once, I went after my roommate
       with a beerbottle, was restrained.
       That morning he, nor I —
       no one fuckt her,
       & the story dies
       like an empire rusting in its scabbard.

ix   Onward we go,
riding into the sexual dark.
Lot, Pellinore, Gareth,
Gawain – our pricks
remembering Arthur's seed. To Uther,
his father, there was no other grail
than Igraine's womb. Disguised
as her husband, he enters. How
we all dream of that moment.
The rapist's glamour.

For afterward she loves him.
The husband, they find,
has been conveniently killd
in the night. Their child
king of Britain.

x   Dreaming of begetting Arthur. Spawning monuments
to the prick that stirs, violence, love.

xi   This, enslaved us:
knights, with lances chasing grails –
ladies, cloisterd in castles & lakes.
& the knights beating down the gateways
& Arthur at last
sailing off on his barge into the water.
Generalizing, militarizing,
the sexual roles,
the women posted to hearth & bedroom
the men to pens in council chambers,
swords on Mt Badon.

xii   Making Elayne a modern women, who forced
Lancelot to play
by the men's rules? Wielding her cunt
like the dishes Maggie
hurld at Jiggs –
also Margawze, later Gwenevere?

xiii So you seduced me early that July.
I was 22, with steel plates
on my shoe heels, driving
a Triumph sports car, dreaming
of having you perhaps
in August.
              In September writing
'Lie back & yield
woman, Margawze,
or kneeling
crouching over him,
dance on it in the moonlight
thou holy mosochist
– the flesh-contorting eruption –
the death of kings!'

xiv Killd by his own prick.
Arthur, fucking his half-sister,
begetting Mordred. The woman's
revenge. The way to a man's heart.
Arabella throwing a pig's dork at Jude.
Hiding eggs between her tits as he unwittingly
chases her to bed.

& you. Imagining yourself pregnant
four months running, & in the fourth
scaring your own blood from its flow
until our wedding day.

xv   As a child you playd
      at gymnastics with a girlfriend's
      father, learning
      envy. When your breasts came, you
      & a boyfriend competed weekly
      at lifting weights in his parents'
      basement. Power.
      You thot that everyone wanted,
      power, flexing your biceps, painting
      your eyes. At the gymnasium
      I could not keep you
      from the punching bags. At parties
      you taunted the men to wrestle, begd
      to be tosst, beaten.

xvi   I tell you the sword
      will be rusting, your own hands,
      your fingers be rusting,
      your heartbeats, you will hear them
      being consumed, hear
      thieves in that countinghouse
      laughing.

xvii   Mordred, born:
    & Arthur, told by Merlin
    only that his slayer
    is a babe that May,
    continues to die, gathering all
    the knights' & lords' children
    of that month
    – 4 weeks old & less –
    setting them adrift in a ship
    to wail, & die.

    The 'flower of chivalry' –
    fuck the women, murder the babes.

xviii   Dying the death of Arthur, emblazoning
    my initials on books, on manuscripts
    of poems, telephone
    memos. Swaggering
    to your door with chocolates,
    flowers. Playing the classroom
    like theatre, the teacher on horseback.
    Writing jokes, for poems.
    Writing poems, for love. & you.
    Thinking to have married a king.

xix That's me, the lion
     fangs closed by a woman's hands,
     claws fixt to the ground
     by her dull green eyes.

xx   While Merlin waits
     entombd alive in the cave.
     Merlin, whose eyes could read blackness,
     whose hands alterd faces, moved castles, lifted
     mountains. Whose powers as children we mimickt
     & envied. As adults schemed for. Prayd.

     Whose pride we would also share, as he rejects
     sorcery as a way
     to Nineve's bed,
     preferring love. Chivalry.

     & she rides beside him thru the forest,
     making him 'good chere
     tylle sche had lerned of hym
     all maner of thynges,'
     her tits jouncing, her smile
     reminding of the lips below.

     Then the cave. A metaphor?
     Nineve proposes. Merlin enters,
     for love. & so he is trapt,
     trapt forever, the girl
     returning the 'grete stone' across the entry?
     locking a word across the passage?

xxi   So long to realize what
         the grail was. Particularly,
         not you. Instead, mounting up,
         following Lancelot
         into Gwenevere's bed.
         Watching her flirt with Mellygraunce, lie
         to Arthur.

xxii   The uterus
           'largest muscle
         of the body, far heavier
         ... than the powerful biceps
         of a heavyweight champion prizefighter'
         says Guttmacher. Cf. Nineve.
         Elayne. Gwenevere.

xxiii   Lancelot & Gwenevere. How near
              we came to their sainted.
              love. I
              treasured you as if
              you were a scabbard
              of spun gold. Spinning
              gold. & you?
              clutcht me –
              like a Dresden figure for your mantel.
              Back & forth I rode there, flying
              banners. soliloquizing. glaring
              thru my porcelain eyes.

xxiv   Forget the whole
              book, I tell you – even
              Morgan le Fay, not
              not at all 'liberée'
              or would that be your
              big thrill, if a witch
              a sorceress? –
              holding knights
              for lovers
              in your castle dungeons

xxv   What is, the association between Elayne
(Elaine? Eleanor? Helyn?) & the literal
grail? It, the gold cup carried
to Britain by J. of Arimathea, is fertility —
fertility put to its right use — healing,
the restoring of lands, the turning of men
from lechery, blood-letting, armtwisting etc.
Cornucopia.

& Elayne. Who wins Lancelot for two nights
by enchantment: the first
on her father's command to beget
the knight to release the grail. OK
But the second. Lust? Power? Risking
not only discovery by Gwenevere but
the betrayal of the latter's adultery. & so Lancelot
suddenly a madman, escapes naked
thru the thorn bushes, while
in the passageway the two women
scratch? spit?

xxvi   Sir Balan rides
thru forest, thru wasteland.
Bands of armed men
lurk in rocks, in chapels,
charge with spears to slay him.
He does not hear their names
or see their faces.
Only their shields, shining.
Some, he runs thru with his spear, others
unhorses, laboriously dismembers,
hours with his sword. All
he must kill. behead, identify.
Their bodies lie behind him
on his trail like discarded
signposts. Not
a good life. Only his blood-tipt sword
pointing onward.

xxvii   Shortly after midnight, I
        alone in the house watching
        a late movie. Over the soundtrack
        I had heard the open exhausts
        of the car approaching
        too fast — race on
        toward the hilltop corner.

        I arrived at the wall as the dust
        still floated. The back of the seat
        had moved him forward,
        the steering wheel, back.
        I could see an ear-ring chaind
        to the rear-view mirror,
        but not his face. For his blood
        lay on the inside of the shatterd windows
        emulsified with moonlight, engine oil.

xxviii But how could I be Sir Lancelot,
        who wins gratitude
        for battle, welcome
        to an enemy's tower.

        Led down corridors
        of sweating stone, stuttering
        candles. The bedrooms remote,
        dark. The lady

        already naked in the bed,
        or coming to him, silently,
        in the night. So that often
        he wakes to find her only after

        they have loved. Should he?
        Have refused? Is she lady? Maid?
        Wife? Daughter?
        Is is blackmail, love, she wants?

        Marriage? Miraculous child?

xxix   So I quit – would not
fight duels for you, invade kitchens,
playrooms, not screw
all your housewife girlfriends.

I hated him, your Christian Arthur,
murdering his children in Chittagong
fucking his sisters at Oweri.

xxx   Can't you see
where it all leads? Arthur
driving his spear thru Mordred's body
the son, thrusting himself up on the shaft
to axe
his father. Both
playing it straight. A faithful
re-enactment of the son's incarnation, & still
continuing – women like you, Margawze,
lusting to be duped, beaten,
taken; suckers
like me.

xxxi   Breasts encrusted with jewels,
         a clitoris of gold: our
         Gwenevere, cloisterd
         with her Avon
         lady.

xxxii   Trying to start with an idea.
         You with your fashion mags,
         the Kama Sutra.

         & then at the movie house we watcht
         Lancelot. You admired
         his flourish drawing
         his sword. Gwenevere too admired,
         all the old puns, his couching
         his lance, thrusting his poignard.
         Or so argued
         the director, keeping an old
         king alive. thinking like you. Boned
         levers.
         Stainless steel shoes.

xxxiii   It's like Erysichthon who cut himself
chopping down a tree.
Or like you, & Gwenevere,
starved yourselves —
of food, love.

xxxiv   & remember how Arthur
(also his court ladies) lamented
the questing of his knights
for the grail. & how I
spent two years at your wish
keeping our lives from my books,
& elsewhere how the Borghia popes
built palaces, or how Cleveland,
Hamilton, Chicago, Detroit,
poisoned the Great Lakes water. That
was Arthur. Not dead. Poisoning our blood
too, inflaming our brains
with heroes, palaces.

xxxv   Prick, cunt — my god, not
weaponry. Please, if you forget
the King of Swords, he will die.
Then the dish, the cup
will bear water, & even the staff
stand, sprout leaves, branches.

xxxvi   & the death of Arthur continues.
His knights, your knights
joust tonight in Belfast,
lead armies, now, August 21, 1971,
in Bengla Desh, Sudan,
have begotten, ten years in Saigon
100,000 orphans of chivalry.

xxxvii   Wounded in the thighs. The euphemism.
King Pelles. King Mordrayns. A low
blow. Your tongue first,
complaining of – ineptitude. & lack
of love. Like the thorns Lancelot
plunged between, to madness; Gwenevere,
her 'barbd' tongue.

Then your leaving. No words for it
now, but the months afterward
waiting for the lady. Mary's blood
on Christ's face, the womb
on the altar, a chalice gleaming.

xxxviii   Sitting by the window watching the walnut
leaves bloom. What had they to do, with you,
you askt. Preferring your stufft dogs & bears.
Your summer dresses arrayd in the closet. Then
there was Gwenevere, displaying her gown beside
the lists. What do you think of her? Did you
ever read of her preparing meals, bearing children? Healing her servants at Corbyn? Feeding
them at Sarras, at Corbenik?

xxxix   We also remember
Joseph of Arimathea. Not
for his plume, armourd horse.

Carrying the goblet
to a place where a river
returnd its waters to the sea.

& Mary's cup
inverted, ran down Christ's side
with mercy.

My new love's belly too
becomes, with care,
a cornucopia

as I watchd it thrust
not steel, but our blood, out
into the breathing air.

xl   Corbenik.
'Cor benoit', blessed
horn.

George Bowering
Allophanes

I

The snowball appears in Hell
         every morning at seven.

        Dr Babel contends
about the word's form, striking
its prepared strings
          endlessly, a pleasure
moving rings outward thru
             the universe. All
       sentences are to be served.

You've tried it & tried it
           & it cant be done, you
cannot close your ear –

          i.e. literature
must be thought, now.

        Your knee
        oh
        class
        equal
          poet
will like use a simile because he hates
ambiguity.

        The snowball says it:
all sentences are imperative.

II

The culture
        tastes just like roast pig.

Here in what are not,
              never were, the 'Outer Continents'

      where the buried ikons
are scattered throughout the soil we walk over,
paths hardly worn.

              Myths communicate
              with each other, & men
              seldom find out.

              The writing finger moves on
              & the sentence continues.

Archaeology is random, snow castles
are alright for lyric poems.

Being ventures us. A stolen base
wasnt there before you reacht it.

          Now it is real as a newspaper
              headline in Hell.

III

Fold the page before the ink dries
    & read before you pass on.

    Literature must be thought now.

There is no perspective
    when the eye is transparent.
When the author dies
    I disappear.

Companionship is true growing up,
    I reach for the companionship of art.

•

Ego dominus teus ? Oh, yeah, who are you?

'I am thy god of love.'

        Teh! I do not love litrachure,
        books are my companions,
        we grow old together,
        we will never meet in Hell.

        And you think *this* life is lonely!

Among earth, sky, mortals, divinities,
the obscure lies necessary to the luminous,
to make seeking take place of the random,
random, passive, the mental, lose it, Bubby,
spirits rejoice!
    the snowball is not the cold.
The free-standing flame is seen in the pool
you enter with your last wet page.

The work is henceforth

the author dead

the book, beside you

a face of the world

to which it was always leading

IV

Literary deciphering is not clarified butter.

By the help of an image
I call to my own opposite, summon all
that I have handled least, least lookt upon.

Have a seat on my language,
& here we go,

lecherously, thru the flowing world
of Hera's clitoris.

With a neo classical
Neal Cassady, what a driver!

How do we get from the north pole
to the south pole?

& what would a snowball
know about polar knowledge?

Drive right past that lady, that's
St. As Is.   No, lady, sorry, my mother
says I gotta come home write a god damn poem.

Look, the big fellow just served her
some *coeur flambé.*

If you speak in tongues this trip, companion,
may I listen in ears?

V

'Talk to me of originality
and I will turn on you with rage.'

Open me not to find a beating heart
but the irregular book of my people.

Hell is filled with those who have
lost the good of the intellect.

Lost their *parole vide,*
unable to serve their sentences in the dark.

Whatever I learned has run wild.

I awake in a hospital
under a patchwork quilt.

I underwent the operation of language
& wake in the recovery room.

As the colours stitch together
before my eyes.

As St. Arte is my bedside nurse

in a snow white skirt.

VI

I havent got a Dante's chance in Hell.

That snowball's got red stitches
& it's imitating God.
Tells me from third to home
is The Way Down And Out.

(Aw poet, just tell us how you
felt about something.)

What?
You dont want the untying
that frees the mind?

Dionysus is the power in the tree.
— like a Louisville Slugger.

There is safety in derision,
read either way.

Sacredness of the act of thought
is transferred to the record, books made from trees,
& there it is, unmelting literature.

(Oedipus at Kelowna)

I woke to find the others gone,
six men working round the camp,
& I alone inside the tent,
I alone to meet the boss.

I'm too far north to run into the wood
where wisdom floods out work & fear.

VII   (labour, life, literature) (the gods)

Keeping your eye on Satan's dewlap
    you seek my complicity (

            And when, amid no earthly moans
            Down, down that town shall settle hence,
            Hell, rising from a thousand thrones,
            Shall do it reverence.

) in this watching
in this (?) madness

                        / Hermes & Aphrodite
                        face to face
                        coupling again
                        on the far side
                        of the moon

        I have loved you better than my soul
        for all my words, else why be we here?

        You'll join in burying my poem
        at some crossroads.

                    Aw narrative
                    is a telling blow.

                    Tell the story of men,
                    their progress on Earth,
                    a cancer on her body.

This is depressing salt I stand in, I sink.

The egg sits there,
it does not rot itself.

Watch the three-year-old
walk thru the gate
carrying her own lunch bucket.

A burden I cant stand to carry
as I must rattle my head & body
to break the pictures of my
cooperating, dying father.

An other, that close,
an other, &
that near, an other.

& where has Maud gone?

Here I am,
all over.

She crouches
over the fire,
her back curved
to her care,

child watching
from his wrappings
in the dark.

VIII

Does not the eye altering alter all?

It is a spilled ice cream ball,
kick it to hell & Gone,
& turning the cone over,
place it on your head.

Stay aboveground that way.

You get a head-ache &
          germs scatter to the ends of the earth,

Oh sages standing in God's holy shit.

IX

How embarrassing, said Mr Auden
    finding himself still awake at midnight.

The traffic control operator in Byzantium
always takes time for lunch
to munch the cooled flesh
of some gray sheep.
                The one oclock gong
just tells him what time it is.

            The dead are breathless
            & so am I
            alive

            going at times
            where they are.

            Strange names,
            a phonebook of the damned.

Vein frenzy awoke & he died.

The winds scatter fragments of the exploded gods.
Fall leaves blowing about one's feet.
Cross yourself.
Burn the books.

Desire is not hunger,
       desire makes it impossible to eat anything.

I will always want to open a veil before beauty one day

& next day melt it down with coarse salt.

           (pluck the melting sno-cone of the lightbulb)

X

Et verbum cano factum est .

A large invisible hand is spinning those wheels Ezekial sees.

But the flesh became chops.

History, history, its range adds to our being,
not our knowledge, history
is a shadow of myself cast upon the stream of time.
The world's meaning is the shadow of the gods,
passing one another, in commerce, in furious battle.

Those cast out are without shadow, without words.

      See the word made white & melting
      before the turn of the fiery wheel.

      I see the dog licking it up,
      he turns & goes home, cano mirabilis.

      — I do believe that Eblis hath
      a snare in every human path —

The world's meaning is exactly
fol de rol de rolly O .

(Put the contraries
back into mortal life,

fail at suicide,
barely.

— burn the books
burn the books

Stamp the snow off your boots
onto the face of the rug.

XI   (the egg-ziled gods)

(Run for the roundhouse, Nellie, he cant corner you there.)

Sea spray crashes on the temple
     & sets it aflame.

         Wear your best suit
              when you jump into a volcano.

You would sweep me away
into an indefinite world
that fills me with terror!

Shuffle: courage & power
       knowledge & pleasure

          fire

air   water

                  Al 'Chemical' Rose
                  has quick hands
       earth   & a strong throwing arm

XII

There is no system, Al Rose falls into an easy chair
brought for relaxation into the laboratory.
His thought threatens him, it is
the perilous deterioration of dynamite.
It is the pattern of snowballs
thrown against a maroon wall.

                Dionysus crucified on a wheel,
                stupefied in a Kelowna vineyard.

His gods speak no man's language,
what arrogance, the churchmen would hear their 'voices.'
One sees their messages in the reeds.

Read his thoughts as experts sift thru an airplane's wreckage

                Oh God, let's have war, fuck art, that
                phony lastingness, shoot him in the belly,
                blood is vintage, there'll be another
                crop, the vines will plunge into
                the earth, fanatics will raise another.

                Why should men die & books live?

  •

On TV we sat breathless as death,
        watching them blast the top off the mountain,

to begin, to make a perfect earth, a perfect smooth black orb.

I had gathered about me all gods
                because I believed in none.

Every time the peacock raises the mirror breaks
                in 'numberless' pieces & the world
                must be re-distilled.

If you dont understand the story you'd better tell it.

Damn a people who cant handle or be handled
        by more than a single god. Those slaves, those wisps.

XIII

Do you believe all this stuff?

Man & the unthought are contemporary.
The unthought is not born of him or in him
but beside him.

Forget Hell,
            Heaven must be another, a camisole,
            must be what we dont want.
            What I want is baseball, jazz, & Viennese food.

            Credo quia absurdus sum

            Take off your shirt & let the sun burn.

My soul grows larger as it rolls downhill,
beauty grown sad with its eternity.

Thus.   Logos is true narrative,
wild logos, mad skier, Al Rose intent on suicide,
his meaning left in lines on the melting snow.

            The iconoclast preaches in his best clothes,
            the pedagog levels a burp-gun at his jacket buttons.

XIV

Al Rose: I have little reason.
Bachiller: To what?
A: What?
B: Little reason to what?
A: To wit.

A: History is the spirit made concrete.
B: With the odd window.
A: The odd balcony.

A: Is the self always gathering the undone to itself?
B: Yes.
A: No, it is always moving into the other,
    removing its clothing as it goes.
B: You're only interested in the narrative of philosophy.

A: Yes.   *9*
B: Odd.

A: It takes time to centre in on a moving target.
B: I've never been moved much by a target.
A: To aim straight & tell the truth, that is our first virtue.

B: Nowadays we talk often of a gift, but with no idea of a
    giver.
A: & teachers?
B: There is only learning.
A: Thoth was the great giver.
B: What we have is not a gift but a possession.
A: Yes, I suppose so. An image Monday.

XV

Hieros   (marry, liquify)

Nothingness is a point   Hear a
of departure. Choose becoming   dead face
over being, how do elsewise   laughing
& love thyself?   centuries ago,
                                          your kinsman.

The Doom of the Powers: all the planets
                                drop into the Sun.

Geronimo makes a great catch against the wall
        & it melts in his hand.

& you think you can talk to the gods
    in English?

Man is nature, devouring,
man is culture, fueling language

filling the hopper.

The culture tastes like well-cookt pig,
the black pig in the valley.

[Prose Gloss: The numbing explosion of human population
in the past decade has drawn God away from
each man's need. How would the devils find
the time to struggle over every soul?]

XVI

The Holy Gobbler

Morphemes fall in flames from the tree.

There was black fire writ on white fire,
    the poem blazed before my very eyes.
I wanted to dive into the flames,
    save my furniture,
    rescue my 'beloved books.'

Al Rose speaks seventy languages fluently,
    sings in seventy languages,
    his words fall into the sun, athanor
too.

        He looks away from the blaze
        & a black fire meets his gaze.
        A burning tree,
        that speaks thru thee.

Bachiller says oh he is busy bullshitting about Heaven
& his pants are on fire. You watch,
you'll see him sitting in the snow.

God's holy name is at anyone's fingers,
any scrambler,
thank you, Mr Underwood.

XVII

  Only dry or drying sticks can be tied into a bundle.

 He's ninety years old & he sits reading in the pitch black night

B: Pass him by, he's trying to do a number on us.
A: He'll freeze to death, he obviously needs help.
B: He gets heat the same place he gets light to read by.

A: I lookt down his throat & there was the whole universe!
B: His head was then above it.
A: Or cast out of it.

'What matter that you understand no word!
Doubtless I spoke or sang what I had heard
In broken sentences.' The snowball appears
in Hell every morning at seven, fears
no fire more than time, the planets too
will fall into the sun & so will you
& so will you.

    No place on Earth
    is the centre of the world,

    it is the centre of the world.

XVIII   The fruitful void. Athanor.

One said he's been 'trying to learn to use words
& every attempt is a wholly new start.'

Where else may we find our beginnings
but in the language? The shepherd's song
on a hillside in the invaded sub-continent.
That native blows a pipe in our nature.
One is not born alone, one borrows the earth,
a clay, formed anew. A language filled again
in an oast heated from an ancient flame.

                    Build, though,
                    with snow,
                    blow language
                    nummular
                    at the flame.

When you've finisht with them words
throw the skins on the compost, will ya?

That is composition,
autobiologist.

                    The last kiss
                    is given to the void.

                    Bye bye, sweetheart.

        Rome
        was once the biggest city in the world.

        Goodbye, Rome.

XIX *factum*

<u>A little devotion</u>

The spool turns faster the moment you begin to take your eyes off it

You slow it by watching.

>   — Thought is the action of the moment brought —
> But it will take its time,
>   it will take no more time than it would.

          (That is the fine étude of man.)

Pure poetry has no presence
    but only its own being

250 years ago tomorrow
     man stept out of nature
       into history

Ideas fall,
peanut shells
blown by passing vehicles
along the gutter.
         Dog turds
         discolouring the snow
         about them.

         A radiance.

Aw busker,
what dance is this
you tap before us?

                    Only, again 'only'
                    the true beginning of
                    language is poetry.

            Actualité.

XX

Where is the theology in all this?

There will be no recurrence of the pre-
reflective time of man,
        no recourse there,   (That him
          the fine étude   with the
of man walkt with him   big dick?)
        the moment he could stand.

               'Neither baseball
               nor poetry
               is for fun.'

Die, aspiration,
let the man bend over,
make a snowball,
           joyful weapon made of water.
           A kid's jape.
           For the love of God.

Life & art are consubstantial.
      H.C.E.
      lives & lives & lives
      reflected in the mirrors
      along the wall.

Text, Criticism, & Notes.   Edited by George H. Bachellor.

XXI *Simon Magus*

Looking for an oblate snowball
on Eggs Isle.   Inside the real
composing.
          A permanent place down in the universe
over which history
has no dominion.

                    This is not going,
anywhere, not going,
anywhere, not,
going, I dont seem to be,
going. Anywhere.

Exile & cunning. I flew
in my dream, night by night, standing
upright.

                    I had no religious instructors,
                    poor child, only a grandpa
                    who'd once abandoned
                                        the ministry.

               (They've already printed
                    the date of your death.

                    You wont be ready,
            you'll say you have things to do,
                 you'll say it cant be done today.
                    He'll say that's what they all

    say.)

                              I abandoned
    the mystery.

    I keep trying to bite my pencil with a tooth gone five years ago.

XXII

'He does what is done in many places;
what he does other
                    he does after the mode
of what has always been done.'

Not seeking to under
stand this world

                                        (I am making)

but to put his hands
          into it, to continue
                    shaping what he is.

•

'Chemical' Rose:

          His athanor was raised to lips
& lips at that First Supper.

          His familiar pranced beneath the board
ready to retrieve angelic orts.

          His dream lay on a carvèd plank
dropping petals into a cup.

          His tongue drips berry juice
onto his clean shirt front.

          His name is, discovered to be
Huckleberry Finnegan.

XXIII

I felt something strike me.
I fell on something.
With a shape something like my own.

The language
is not spoken,
it speaks.

Somewhere in the world you could have a green rose.

Language scales the real, & continues, on.

Oistrakh
touches
the fifth
string.

Move out of these too tight clothes
when you feel the trance ending

& I will tell you

history is a thing. A dead language
in which all words
describe, & refer,

you may understand history because you made it.

You will never understand nature
         because you are nature,

                              (Jan Garbarek,
                              blow.)
when you are able to shape the natural
         history will vanish from your mind.

Drama
         may not be superimposed.
                              It opens
before your chary feet.

                    Watch, that priest
               looks up at us,
         a snowball wouldnt melt in his mouth!

XXIV   Diaspora

'All imaginable relations may arise between a man and his God.'

What off
was Thoth
but ne'erdowell
exprest.

          Skill forgotten with age.
          Oh dread!   what enters
          to fill that space?

(Shit, shore up the fragments
for yourself, dont expect
a fullness here, I'm only
one pair of ears.)

          The effacement of words.
          History is full of holes
          thru which we may hope
          to escape   (?)

The artist has disappeared,
he is standing silent before God.

Wha'd you say? asks the latter.

I know, I know.
it's all beautiful.
Tell me what we said on it.

The bapdismal font
is full of words.

What fire forms
friday
theism?

Nature
to adventure
prest.

XXV

Here hope is always thwarted.
The future when we get there
     is always other than we'd thought
          & it is not the future.

               Say to it:
'I trust the sufferings endured in battle
     more than I trust you.'

Today we go always to children's games & songs
to prove the real.
                    To try to drown poor pussy cat.

●

The blue fell,
the green rose

& I was prest between.

I lifted & threw something.
It struck something.
& fell in pieces on something like itself.

prose summary: The words proveth the Almighty the
                    greater thing to come along as yet.

XXVI Dispersoid

Pri,   mord,   Eos,   reality
    not the light brim again
        rather sink
            into the ooze

but she pulls
    she weeps
        we are really (surprise) gone from her
        but she weeps

            We see her
                weeping
                    we are there
                        too

Bye, Mama
    we are engaged.

        Language rings us.

There was first the beauty of fucking.
Then the morality of fucking.
Now the fucking drama.
          Here is the theology in all this.

          It has melted in my hand.

          Call me Mister Warm.

Roy Kiyooka
The Fontainebleau
Dream Machine

'over the princes of delirium
over the paupers of peace'

for
Dave Barrett
Angela & George Bowering
Gerry Gilbert
Carole Itter
Sadikiichi Hartmann
Yasuo Kuniyoshi
bp nichol
Wilfred Watson
Phyllis Webb
Georgio Vasari &
Sarah Sheard

out of the lair of breath the Dream

Machine slipt its moorings
in the Cave of my mouth and climbed the tree
tops of my sleeping eyes up into
the cool blue Night   Mother mute mother
of my breath the unvoiced Cry of
the child I am rings the Changes in
your granite mouth

these stones these stones embody a tongue
tied Speech

the 1st Frame shows
Breath (shadowing) Dream (shadowing) Air (shadowing) itself

while the Three Graces adorn the hem of the dream I fall into
all the dreams breath can hoist go up into the sky!
while the three of them unravel the hem of the dream I became
all the figures they unravelled danced on my eyelids high above the
Nile.
then when they began to knit another dream from my unravellings
all the dreams I ever fell thru fell into my astonishment.
Voila! Voila, the air of the Andalusian dog stroking his genitalia

the 2nd Frame shows
all the dreams breath abides betrothed to the Queen of Hearts

the billowing Cloud / Figures swirling

around the Dream Machine's ascent owe their Chiaroscuro
to Raphael and Michelangelo . awesome portent –
or it's that prehensile primate Hero of a Thousand Days a
Mickey Rooney standing on his tousled head waving –
'Golden Hallelujahs' by Metro-Goldwyn Mayer .
'Monsieur, I salute you' acknowledges the Aureole around the Dome
of the Sistine Chapel . the dream always wins in the end
deserve your dream.

the 3rd Frame hides
the Morning Star under the Cowl of Breath

at the Portal of a Dream the

great bald Eagle carries a banner in its claws across
the Dreamer's Threshold . the Dream with its
intricate Flotation-System hovers – motion less – above
the Glacial Plains *etched* on the Shining Metal of
your eyes . at the Port of Dreams you never need a Passport
ask the Eagle, 'who dreamt you?'

the 4th Frame

a Clap of Thunder marking the Distances we travel by Night

High Noon at the base of

the tall *fluted* S T O N E *breath* Column
– a man with a Nikon F-2 measures
the Lattices of Sunlight falling across broken Statues
of a 'once upon a time there was ..! O
the intricate marble fluted Foliations   the
inflamed Lyre ... kindling
                                    stone : leaf : grief

the 5th Frame hides
the actual length of the Column inside your inner Ear

the eye of the Camera Obscura

Lukas Fantuzzi found himself looking thru
an optic Nerve a Verb 'to be' –
projecting pellucid Nouns clowning upside down
inside the dreamer's dormant
Machination . Jewels ...? well why not
jewels worth the Heft of a Maharajah afloat
on the cool blue fountain of our
peregrine A B C's

the 6th Frame exposes
the Retinal Ghost our Host 'Dancing in the dark'

how almost elegantly They stand

at their ease to either side of the dream's Cornucopia
with one hand on their crotch the other claspt
behind a wreath of incised leaves the ingenuous reflection/s
of their hands and breasts a *navel* among flowers.
how the eye opens and closes on the intricately cut Diamond
of their Vows as the unseen air caresses the dream up
from under their marble feet ... I fell into the beguiled air
of their astonishment

the 7th Frame shows
the Hand of the unseen Poet turning into a Palimpsest

sifting the Rune/s for

the Behemoth of Speech: the absolute truth
of those huge white tusks curving in the moonlight marsh
a million years ago ... today. searching the Sahara
for the Algebra of Awe Rimbaud wept when he stumbled on them
in front of the pygmy king's palace. the impossible
death of Chairman Mao on late night cablevision. nuclear
fission. Herr Hermann Göring & Separatism. on the
tusk of a dream I beheld the Elephant standing on the Promenade:
his inflamed ear thrums the mammalian silence

the 8th Frame hides
the real pigeon shit spatter'd on the back of a bronze Napoleon

of the Guardian Mother & her entourage

of Shining Angels: of such Heavenly Hosts I know nothing
but how they seem to be forever suspender'd among gilded clouds
on the back of a hackneyed horse with dangling hooves awry.
lucky or unlucky the Augury they propose lifts a blanket of doubt
from the green morning meadow filled with braying donkeys.
'I would etch a Silvery Horse on the Shining Metal of your eyes ..'.
the Dream whispered, dying, into the dew under their cloven
feat . replete replete the dream dies ... into

the 9th Frame hiding
the unspent Heat of the Solar Belfry, the climbing plant I am

step lively up to the door cut into

the wall Flaming Wall of Figures falling with
all the dreams breath enlivens dying on their forked tongues.
steep'd in the intricate Gyrations of an imagined hell
they preside over the diurnal Wave of Fire falling*
into the river's Mouth, O Harbour! step quietly but firmly thru
the door way of your incredulity where all the dreams
death remainders lie in the folded Silt under a Mute's tongue.
O the unrepenting Snake coil'd in Cleo's brazen hair!

the 10th Frame hides
the fluted *breath* Column in the unmined Quarry under
your tie'd tongue

the man tipping his top hat is not Fred

Astaire or Jacques Cousteau.
the Dream Machine ascends or descends according to the precise
calculus of ancient Taoists or, Mandrake the Magician
pulling a Tableau of Writhing Figures out of his adroit sleeve on
Cabal a Vision. O the tiny pair of eyes peering through the
slats of a Venetian blind... the heap of butts we left behind in
the burnt-out Colosseum. 'SVB PENNIS EIVS TVTV ERO!' cried
the Angel-Maker, as the Dream rose out of an acid bath, burnish'd
in its own Mysterium

the 11th Frame hides
the Butterfly Wing tattoo'd on the Ceiling of your Mouth

under the charade of clouds the still wind-rudders

Disturbed by the Slowly Turning Propeller of Adamant History
under the intricately-pleated Shroud – a Tinderbox
of Prophecies fall into the fire fueling the belly of an insane
Dream. stirred by the slowly turning propeller 'People
want History to resemble themselves. or, at least to resemble
their dreams. happily they sometimes have great dreams.'
be-stirred by the slowly turning propeller both Charles de Gaulle
& Felix Nadar are pseudonyms for the unassailable Ghosts
dancing a jig in the heart of the undreamt dream. at the Potsdam
Summit Meeting Joe Stalin turned to the stalwart general –
'Death, my friend, Death always wins in the end.'

Death is the Slowly Turning Propeller stirring
the 12th Frame

for the un-dreamt vowel

in Night's Unfolding/s

the Dream Machine & its ghostly twin the undreamt dream
ride the Night Mare Sky above Pristine Towers
Gleaming Thrones of a Corrosive Economicks pitch'd on steep
Medieval rooftops – indentur'd to the Medici with
their Midas Touch. ask the bronze Eagle pointing towards
a Labial Sunrise about the un-ballasted air trap't
in a dead man's throat ... the Dividends you pay through the nose
for   my permeable Friend

the 13th Frame shows how
obliquely Shadow/s fall across the face of so-called Skyscrapers

Eugene Delacroix noted in his journal

How he felt more like fucking her this morning:
every time this happens another nail is driven into the coffin
of Colour Symbolism . there's nothing new under the sun
pouring through my loft window nothing but getting a huge
hard-on and/or painting her radiant Visage . ask
Amadeo Modigliani what happened when he drove the last nail
in that awe-filled coffin? the Eye in the loft &
the Tatter Dream *Monitor the Daily Beneficence*

the 14th Frame shows
the Dream's Effluvia pouring into the Gutter of a Song

while the imported Italian sculptor chip't

a Way through the last bits of wood clasping Aphrodite's heel
the spent Dream Machine kissed the cool cobblestones .
when the Air ravishing Her lifted her arms up to the wind All
the children playing *hide and go seek* whistled a loud .
O City Fathers giving Caesar yet another statute –
your parenthetical airs leave even these oak trees leaves
speechless:

the Air the air a round the dream obscene/ Splendide!
the 15th Frame pre-figures
the Pulp of an Unborn Dream buried inside the Book of Lawes

l'aura of the Ukraine Opal Alberta the

Carboniferous Sky over Europa. and Asia: Black
as my horse Sleepy Jim who fell thru
the winter sod roof of our Root Cellar & ate ate
til the snow the Snow falling thru the hole
the huge Sky-hole he had fallen thru fell down on
top of him: Black as his bloated belly his
Nest of mash't-up roots. we tore out the whole front
of the cellar to bruise him an exit –
and chained behind the tractor dragged Jim thru

> aphasia a cross the frozen stubble
> aphasia of his Famine
> aphasia the drifting snow-mantl'd pasture broke n
> aphasia down   the huge hole
> aphasia black root *pie* in the sky

> aphasia . . .

the 16th Frame shadowing
the Inflamed Lyre burning in the 2nd Narrows

the end of dreaming is the beginning of

D a y G l o w C o l o u r s spinning a Shiner on
your astonished eyes : Daughters my Daughters
How? how is it I suddenly *see* G r e e n ; *hear* B l u e
smell B r o w n : *touch* breath of R o t u n d .
what an Epithalamion of Bird Songs Throng my return to
Earth *Beloved Barge Mirage*
                              Port of Call

the 17th Frame belongs to those
who celebrate Night's Libations at *The Mermaid* and *The Cecil*

the Dream dies every morning in the cave

of your Mouth with all the starlings in the pear tree singing
Cantonese . O the Pear Tree in my backyard on
Keefer Street . C h i n a t o w n . my C h i n a t o w n
breathing things I lie under the dream's belly
a goat-footed savant in the Aura of its Commotion/s.
'be me', the Dream whisper'd, 'be my Day Light.'

let the Seances of another day startle ...

the 18th Frame

Sodom
Gomorrah &

Carthage
Await

The Sultan
Sunne

the artist/author of
the Fontainebleau Dream Machine
acknowledges the F.D.U.
(Fellowship of the Dreamt Universe) for
its untiring Collaboration
without which these Texts could not
have been written let alone
collaged

bpNichol
The Martyrology
Book IV

∎

purpose is a porpoise

a conceit

is there a sea

yes

is there a cloud

yes

everything elemental
everything blue

the precision of openness
is not a vagueness
it is an accumulation
cumulous

yes

oceanic

yes &
anything elemental
anything blue is

sky

    sea

       the heart of
the flame

          stories
st orie's domain

             but the french say
'main'

                ti
                    la
                        do
hand

the h &
what else

if the language poses questions
'are there answerers'

what i ad
dress
            clothe in
thot
        not
adjectives for nouns nor
names where things will do

eternally new

a hand shake
speare or sword
the old 's' word
cutting edge of accuracy

if they cannot see
they are blind
                            hear
deaf

            de-
e
    f
-fective

'the divine right of'
the hard left cross
nails the boss's son

we are always pleading
asking for
            forgiveness
favours
            never the old hosannas we used to raise
still worship the wheel in all its i's's
make ourselves   capitals
of earthly doubt
                forgive us

the d will out
as the b drops thru its
half note
            configuration

i is singing scale
i hails you

Hart works the 'e'
reversing the conjunction
finds the d n a
connective
            the heart of
writers & their obsessions

who cares

the oral hang-ups change

a concern for listening

if i let the actual speak
it will reveal itself

admire the form
be seduced by it
as part of
the love of
language

'love me for my mind as well'

elementary statement
elemental state
meant for
            completion
combination

we work
the changes
always
to reveal
lest the actual re-veil itself
a shifting of
the humus
            cumulous covers
poetry's reviled &
spat upon
            sweet spit & hhh of breathing
the old so &
so my dreams are troubled

what matters it the nights are sleepless
i lie awake with poems   hymns
these rhythms
insistent as the brain is
with images
            a pounding in the chest of
words
      the l imposition of the earth
the singular
word + one = world
            i seek
solutions to equations that are already solved?
no!
      only
an understanding
            ((i place myself as less than
what is obviously greater)
            all knowledge
is to know the ledge you stand on
half way between earth & sky
where the clouds slide
form & dissolve around you)

a way of moving in the fluid surely
not as a man who walks in water
where swimming would better do
or as Christ did
                    walking out upon it
to teach them
the stupidity
of rigid category

i want the absolute precision
of fluid definition
the saints learned
long ago
            built their towns
'upon the plains of heaven'
blue of sea
                (sky)
white clouds
                    (land)
intermingling

driving north today
fog giving way to rain
rain to snow
& snow
            covering the road finally
there is no definition
where you cannot see the line
of drawing
                writing
                        music
the form a focus for us
i wakens from
the dreamed landscape

out of the words' tumble
should meaning separate
when it is the torrent sweeps me

thru the bound beeches
the switch
             hits the mind
blood rushing to
the surface of
the skin

         sink
               in

             ink's
                    sin
                        is
no sin
         unless it is the nosin' around
down at the surface where the depth is

we read it in the i's
i centre is a tease
no centre ring at all
Adam knew
the apple was a pull
a way
a separa-
tion-
ning
        the whole for
the part
sin of
partiality
who should have been impartial
(imp art i always wanted to attain
a dance among the little ones)
wanted to be part of
the whole
              flows thru
into the universe
absolute & open
poem of
perfect movement
containment of
the flux

                    the wind outside rises
air
      grey
day
      janvier
moment when the movement changes
the line straightens out & stretches on ahead
there's room to pass
out into the flats of heaven
the cloud land
a night's sleep has seen the last of
for the moment
momentum carries us
on in our arc around the sun
& the lines become as long as the tongue can
                        /carry without breathing in

images shift
                  blue sky turning back to grey

it is the wind moves it

it is a language the celts knew & spoke of

runes
      (the running e's)
pass as vowels thru energy

consonants as nouns

vowels as verbs

what are the sentences that form
words they're made of
syntax of alignment i want to see
apparent in every bush & tree
placement of the sea & land
a plan
            not in the sense of plot
pre-conceived
but there
            readable

if i am able to
see man
        writable
purpose
        breaks skin's surface
gains control
moves from the known   on
into the un
prefix delimiting the road
out of the two year darkness of the mind
no music i could find to lead me
sick of ending things before their time
is marked

                b
eaten up
's sung in
        the bottom range
down the upper
twists of phrase

sur visage
the mouth opens
writing following the o of
sound
        noise
products of the human voice

awaking
too little sleep
snow falls
        beyond the wind
o
    w forms
at the word's end
word's beginning is
the book's end
that conundrum
vision
riddle we are all well rid of
the dull pass of wisdom

w is d
o ma
i'n h and
the me's restated
at the pen's tip's ink
at the tongue's noise
w in d
  din
Blake's vision of
Golgonooza

after noon
the clouds give way to sky
blue
  e
le me 'n
t
 always
why

to rid me of
the ugh in
thought
i spell anew
weave the world
out of the or
binary
   the note spun
out of the dinary into the few
letters i am granted
signs
  to reach who i cannot touch
miles & years between us

february 1 1975 5:48 p.m.
conscious i may be dead when you read this
as two nights ago i lay awake
trying to grasp the concept 'infinite'
a feeling of vertigo
i am so much less than everything
the fact of the all
encompassing me

                    gunning into high
digger digger
the cat gut &
the fiddler
              questions to answer
answer's an A
                    B
ginning
          of the town
the saints came down from
buildings crumbling
middle ground abandoned
the road takes me
into the centre of that emptiness
the past is made by
the present

at root the blue is bleu
means 'bright'
if you get the b right
everything's ginning
essents & essentials
so much of the problem is misnaming

last night
              walking home
stars above the church at the foot of Huron
the sky a darker blue to purple
range i cannot name
that activity
what should be play
too often's re-creation
the change that Langtek worked
'wreck-creation'
foreign to me now
                        i want the world
absolute & present
all its elements
el
    em
        en
            t's

o
  p q
    r

or b d
        bidet
confusion of childhood's 'kaka'
the Egyptian 'KA'
                soul
rising out of
the body of
the language

the streets are not named
standing in the centre square
staring up at windows they no longer gaze from
the whole point of it ended
meanings for existence
                        gone
the stuttered b
              ing
that is living
stammer thru our days
impotent in less obvious ways than
the limp dick or
frozen ocean of
              response
the saints come down to
their mortality
            or fled
to live among the dead
outside our memories
the city they built
a memo re
a son
        one's debt to one's father
forgotten
            farther away than
the next star or
page
        surface that the eye lights on

in the press of speech
awkward words are chosen
that decision is
the voice's prelude
skeletal remains
apparent in
the choice of
building blocks

the 'b' locks into place

a command

in the space left
the weight of air shifts
visible compounds of earth & water
within a balanced sphere of
forces

        fire (which is sun)

        air

        earth & water (clouds)

        air

        earth & water (earth)

        fire (which is core & molten)

we can journey outward
into hell
        the suns & darknesses of space
or inwards
into cave-black liquid stone &
fire
    at the earth's core
old questions i had asked
answered

                    Lucifer fell
from fire onto earth & could not rise again
burrowed into
                    the ground

the meteor in northern siberia
June 30th 1908
                    'a sound was heard
louder than . . . thunder
                            and a column of fire
. . . shot skyward'

'a farmer living fifty miles away
was hit by a heat wave
which he feared would set fire to his clothing'

i burn on the inside
                        unnamed purpose
as i had dreamed it years ago
to write my way thru the books of the dead
let the process take me
thru
        into
the books of the living
& i move now
out of 3
            into 4
or 1
        some new beginning
sensed here
amid the sensory sensation of
speech
            these words
the arch
ark
        Io
logical
            invocation of
the change
                    flames i saw

among the monotones
the burning beasts
                    cattle
Io of the many eyes
Nura Nal's visions
Io who suckled Zeus
& 'invented the five vowels of
the first alphabet
                    & the consonants
B & T'
            Nura Nal who sees thru dreams
what is to transpire
that arch which takes us
over the present
                    into the future
arks we sail
like Noah or Utnapishtim
till we come to that day
no longer young
others come
            as Gilgamesh did
caught up in
the immortality game
to question us

there is noone here to question

the wind howls in the empty streets
shutters bang uselessly
i pick my way thru the remnants of their speech
the crumbling outline of their modes of thot
i am no closer to them
only further away from earth
dizzy from the lack of air
i stumble frequently

in the long hours the heart is slowed
the mind drifts between the particles
letters of the law

the B is born
            one day before
the celebration of your son Lord
according to the Bethluisnion
& i sit
late in the Nth month
waiting for the F to dawn
seven days from now
ash dropping from
the fire i have lit in my hand

the B gins us
A's the birth
tree
day of
        celebration
I
  the death
yew
loss of we
which is our perfect B
ginning
            false pride of individuality

that i am
            yes
but i was of
came from
            this soil
W
   o men
we all begin in
that embrace our M's contained in

the soil forsakes us
                we are lost
Kryptons we all came from

infant crying for our vanished homes
crumble in the face of fragmentary stone
remnants of our origin
shakes us
power's gone
orphaned I's
        brought down to *their* mortality

i hang
suspended in the N which is my name

sequence is the changing of the moon
the month's advancement
B L N
F

am i ly-
ing?

the shrines change hands
the sacred groves' scarred
battle for our gods across millenia
drift in between
never easy with these mono themes
mono theisms
torn between our parents
mother/father
can't i praise you both

i move from streets
into empty corridors
the saints abandoned
long ago
took their separate ways to earth
or outward
        to the stars
other suns & planets
other gods
useless catalogues of sins & longings
'are the two equated?'
'sometimes'
'oh'

the is M
the particular
emblem of the end a
beginning a
w a y
ME/WE
returned to
that vision &
this time
             i write the letters clearly
the w rite of consciousness
a transparency's
too often viewed opaquely
lack of seeing
lack of being
sing
      sang
            sank
froid
      et chaud
caught between the opposites
throats full of praise
masked pleadings with the ones we fear will leave us
kill us
            will us dead & gone
cinq
      six
            sept
mid-initial drop
Set or Seth
whose opposite Osiris
he murdered
             for the sake of Isis
Aphrodite Urania
Aphrodite Erycina
who tore out her lover's balls
in the moment of heat
that cold consumes us

Cain & Abel
the brothers or the twins
jealousy
divides the year
divides the family
mi
    fa
       so
la ti
etude &
longitude a
fixing of points on a grid
language
       where the grid is
no longer apparent
buried in the history of the race
the alphabet
A to Z of
being

the M
the ME
the S is
a way of starting
your feet move hesitantly in the shuttered rooms
the few things they left   scattered on the mantles
artifacts of daily living
rotting garbage that forms their tel
ing
    St Orm   St Reat
St Agnes & St And
St Utter
      who became the town crier
another story
i never bothered to tell
their histories fill my head
as the dead can do

so many years they tried to block out the living
i became their mouth
their breathing
like some misconception of you God
not to illumine the present
but to haze it over
these clouds of the unknowing
false mysteries i railed against
& now they're gone
like the voice of Jung on a distant phone
mumbling
uncritical
i see their faces as they were
jealous of your godhood
your parenting
set themselves up as
better than the rest of us
because we acknowledged our suffering

i preferred St And a clown
human & vulnerable
critical of stupid posturing
absurd hierarchies he'd left behind
aware of the struggle he'd never made
forgetting the common effort raised these spires
built the high-arched windows
placed the cobblestones
lived on
isolate among the many
his face mirrored in the air
he gazed into & fell
self into self
narcosis of narcissus
wandered then
lost among men
the full pain of his loss haunting him

he is gone now
to 'the land from which there is no return'
where Erishkigall holds sway
to Mag Mell
                    the plain of joy
Avalon
            Isle of Appletrees
finally at peace in
the immortality game

in the gardens the trees have died
freed of their artificiality
'in Dilmun the raven utters no cry'

to do what one does
with honour
is the all

ist heal-
ling
        lang
u age
's h
        on
our

        hour

the days are marked by their divisions
purpose
                less divisive in
the long run
lung ran
lang ren
tall
        i is here so
short ly

in bed
2 a.m.
ellie sleeps beside me
images form behind her closed eyes
i am following a line of thot
of ink to
its conclusion

to re member
re articulate
eyes
      mouth
mobility of limbs
in the dream time
connectives vanish
only that one line or link
you seek each morning
takes you back
            e thru k
f g h i j
arcane but logical

here
'where the sea sleeps'
'where the cold is unendurable'
in these 'barbarous lands at
the end of the world'
we are caught in
a tangled dreaming
an immigrant nation of
uncertain history
we are like you saints
the lands we left destroyed
by nothing more than
the hours' passing

tonight
the moon shines
thru this house of glass
as i as well had said it
'the poem is dead
            long live the poem'

i know now the saints were wrong
demigods at best
we have struggled a millenium
without your name
no power to invoke but our own
noun of your being absent
no other nouns cohere

i speak from 'the land of the summer stars'
'at the back of the north wind'
where the souls flock
each spring
the ponds & hills of
dufferin county
set out food at the pond's edge
because it is right & necessary
wander the woods where the old beeches stand
books of your being
light green of new leaves
blue spring sky
that colour range which is the saxon word 'glas'
& it is death i see
which is the absence of the strength to call you
the power to invoke your name
gone in the shifting game of allegiance
your jealous children played
& i am left wanting you
left to amuse myself
mother/father
i am afraid
retreat to theory
talk factually when i feel unsure
hate the noise of such didacticism
hate my hatred of it

journal journey
jour du nalney
move slowly thru the signs of passage

maybe i will ne
ver
    speak a
gain
     mid this
          blue

sky & deep sea
           cerulean

vapour

distant hills

flash of veins
as they show thru
the skin

of constancy
livid as the skin becomes
after a blow

fear or
dismay
the colour of
blood
i dress in
because i am a servant of
words
the colour of plagues
(indecent
         obscene)

'plaid the painter
when hee did so gild the turning globes,
blew'd seas, and
green'd the fields!

yield it all up from
the person
       voice
he hopes is charged with
His blessing

the i dies finally
merges with the land's scape
scope increases
the folded page
writes its way into
the longed for
                    beginning
story
            new
            song
round
        as the lips form

an O
i used to (age 4)
put the period in

early syntax
early speech

you are dead saints
i am half-alive
or better
            some days

calendrical ways

happy in the morning
depressed in the afternoon or

reversals

la tigre

egress

the rest is
written to be written
'it is all so slight'

of hand

the pen's grasped
wrongly but firmly

dreams twist

images erupt

       violent

brush the skin off my head
's oblong

      aluminum

            oblagatto

one word dwelled on
one month

mispelling: 'obligatto'
thinking: 'obligation'
               i am obliged to
play out this path i have chosen
play this tune
write this part as i have just spoken it

because it is necessary

because i am not alone

because to be is cause
(reason versus reasons)
art is to bring together
            join
'lost art of' art –
we are crazy in our isolation
as i am
torn always
so that the truth appears a melodrama when i state it
makes rhetoric of daily speech
'two nations warring in the bosom of a single state'

indispensible

love & hate

essential to
the completeness of the
compo
          sition

moi et me

instrument on which it's played

bound to another

                    obligation

two months to play the theme thru

'you are dead saints'
given back into the drift of print
of speech
                    born anew among the letters
a different tension
                         different reach
of logic
          of the mind's playing out of
reason
          a rhyme
till God's re sonned
on the tongue
the groan that must accompany your birth lord
l or d
          unless the el's read 'one'
one ord er
absolute & true
which is the two tone order of the pun

'one Samuel
              an Irishman
for his forward attempt to pun
was stunted in his stature'
pounded down

(i moved during the course of this writing,
interrupting the patterns, jarring at first
because i found myself, ten years later, back
in the same house i'd lived in during the
writing of 1335 Comox (poem that began
JOURNEYING & THE RETURNS (whose form
was perceived after i moved away from
there (from here))) the dilemma being i
found myself caught up in a) mirror image

(no way to notate the break

caught up in) another
absolute statement for
my mother

(followed the line to come
'air your grievances & longings' with
'a transition taken
                    a return'
& later
              'tonight i kneel
pounded down by the weight of my own resistances
my own fatigue
                    a kind of false pride'
crossed the whole thing out
uneasy with the tone
began this new movement
sudden intrusion of my mother
coupled with a return of self-loathing
'who does not love his words or works'
i saw as
a deeper level of
the pun
stir)

          against the hate of self the love of her

posited

'there is little evidence to support it'

i am
the evidence of
their lovemaking
their spoor

my name is
'little evidence'
little evident in
these proceedings

here in clouds
amid the clash
the roar of
            c's & s's
absence of the loud
                        separator
the same
            i read in in
                        the form of ain
(which is the pain
(mid-initial sequence) or
                        the stain of
sainthood)
            track's a trickle
straight as the jog my memory takes
composed in time the rimes exist beyond the text
contextual
            textural
                        daily bump &
grind
        stripped bare
air your grievances & longings

in these unfinished rooms
pick up the notebook left behind
after book iii
that time i thot
the saints end
                        finally
e nd
        'f eat her

take her away
                in my cap
at dawn
            today
the knowledge
            to d a y
the action i act on'
'her' posited again as
moM/Womom

                        'the change
                        (an
                        angel
                        chang'll
                        hang)
                                    suspended
over my head
suspen dead
deed
        done
one d in
motion
        or one y
changed by
            the revolution

hanged c
revolving r the
credit balance[1]

sense out of nonsense
N on sense
            (which is me)
i spell out changes
realign essentials
as i thot to
sing a balance sing[2]

1 edit with the c r to achieve it
2 agèd
            fall
            /
            n

to make everything the same you say
'nothing is different'

the arguments get obvious

when one's upset one screams

3 or 1?

'it is so unlike me
one like me uses my lungs'

my voice?

                gossip's piss o G.

cloud town's gone down
t into d
artness
then the arkness of her belly

is that the sweat of fear
atlas's salt a
blinding of vision in any case

c as e

'it is all the same'
words one used before

naming things that don't exist

twist

back & forth
                existence only in the naming''
to spawn again in that stream
's forbidden

i cannot rebirth myself
cannot become mine own progeny

(glazed window grey day
you've all gone away
five years since i called your names with surety

i am not the same

(sometimes (at night) i doesn't know who
he is (why? (that's wrong – the sequence
should read w x y – the h interpolated into
the unknown) h is his) not in that old
schizzy sense (i.e. he doesn't know who i is)
but a perception re entity in its entirety ('at
night' because he is all alone & 'sometimes'
because it's accurate) the lacking of a
total
           the problem is in summing up
prematurely (false). he is 31 (yesterday) but
i's what? (joking to a friend he said 'i used to
be 18 to myself but i'm catching up') a question of tension in telling a power in print
opposed to speech

STOP

which is octagonal
h sided
        or
            (an aside

(i's inside
he's an outside face
a pose

a posse or
a nosegay

is it possible
the horses go neigh

posse bull
the whore say

(reintroduction of Blossom Tight, a minor
character from an early draft of a later Captain Poetry poem)

'noone is forgotten we're just rewritten. he's
letting my voice intrude briefly. it's just a
chance for a few laughs at his character's
expense (employing the devices of fiction in
an autobiographical poem)!'

))))

compulsive unmasking

i.e. as opposed to h.e.
over against the french j.e.
so that the sequence reads
h ⎫
i. ⎬   e.(translating) he meaning i
j ⎭
but *not* (capital H) He
— no heresy here
a tic
        there a tickle
statement

'why would you want to make everything the same?'

consistent voice equated with style
                                falsely

style's stylus
the fingers an extension of the mind
ma 'nd me 'nd
                personal history

le monde mundane

mynde & physik

i say 'quoi' mais
je ne sais quoi

it is the i of
histor ⎱
mister ⎰ y

the y's said e
making 'my' 'me'
& 'why' 'whee'
as in wheat or
whyte
        white
                night

stars over Inuvik

walking back from the reading to the hotel
the main streets mud
out on the edge of things
the elements still win
stilts support the town
impermanence shows
120 miles inside the arctic circle you know
we're living out a myth
huddled at the bottom of
most of what is canada
waiting the glaciers return
cities ablaze
fire out of water
burn
        coal/oil/gas
ritual pass of light
gestures against the coming night

here the ravens cry
as they did in Dilmun
raise their wings black against the sky
& fly
        the two we saw
walking thru the brush above the river
Mackenzie flowing north into the Beaufort Sea
'big as a dog they are!
had one once fought a dog in the main street!'

snow falls around us
white on whyte
worlds we have railed against
when will we be
content in the present
moment
   land
whole
   not the part
Ca
 Na
  Da
C 'N D
no space between
the process
   switch
which is the flow
     energy movement of a country

(we woke before dawn, throats dry, remembering then we slept in a desert, frozen tho
it may be, caught between the i & he, am
image of Dilmun in his mind, caught
between first & third person na(ra)tivity)

rising off the tarmack into the sky
looking back along the body of the plane
straining for a glimpse of the arctic ocean
before the clouds close in
      passing thru
into that space between
one layer & the next
not cloud world but another
spectral & strange
     passing thru
into the greyblue
sky over everything

& two days later
driving out of Fort Smith
30 miles to little buffalo falls
ruth rees, ellie & me
watched the water drop
                        60 feet into the basin
the clouds hung grey
for the seventh straight day
as if cloudtown lay in ruins above me
snowbirds flocking up into the sky
trying to make sense of the wreck around me
here in the midst of what has never known city
trace a civilization
                        or what's left of it
looking out over the rapids on great slave river
early the next day
                        the remnants of Fort Fitz
where the great barges lay to
in their journey north to
Hay River   Fort Simpson
whatever outposts sprang up to service those men
lived there
                        north of the Arctic Circle
& i am remembering Dilmun
the empty squares & courtyards
crumbled palisades & steeples
where Utnapishtim lived out his years
& i am wishing i could speak to him
discover how long immortality is
was his city like cloud town
the buildings rearranging themselves daily
the city no enemy ever took
because the streets shift even as you walk them
doorways change
familiar only to the saints who lived there
recognized dwelling signs no stranger'd ever see
they went crazy on this earth
only language retaining the multiplicity they were used to

(typing this out 12 days later i kept coming
back to that line'the edge of things' wondering at the vagueness, knowing what i was
trying to suggest, that my world was finite,
not in imagination but experience, real
limits to what i knew, worried once more
by the tension between process & an ideal
economy of phrase

reading B.S. Johnson earlier this week, dis-
cusses Scott's shift from narrative poem to
novel, what he saw as the death of the long
poem, puzzling its resurgence, its popular-
ity in recent years, i realized the lines had
disappeared between the forms, that the
novel & the poem were merging finally, a
clarity, freedom to move as i choose

                    & later
talking with steve
                        comparing forms
his CARNIVAL
            'my' MARTYROLOGY?
the voiceless voice he saw in Ronald Johnson's poems
i am wary of that impulse within me
would have it out with my i
how can i cast itself out
out of the process i must be true to
is part of the dissolution
                        the disillusionment
create a third person when the i's can't get along?
(jumped ahead
thot 'song'
            son of g
h
   (comes after him)))

the man at the reading said
'how come your poems sound so down?

unlike you?'

(the desire becomes stronger to stretch out,
explain myself, which makes the plain ex,
no longer clear, i want a different ear, a he
like me, a she where the s is (in correct rela-
tion to)
      he/i/she
                 (why is the s the femini-
zer?, makes the i is, births it, gives it its
being, carries the he in the body of its word,
the men inside women, the me in both of
them)

EQUATIONAL DEVELOPMENT: HE/IS/HE

such minimal movements to seek truth in
(steve said 'you'll be accused of shallow-
ness' (hallowness feminized?)))

                            & then?

these clouds are real
mist mister

it's not the saints sing   it's me!

nothing's anything but what it is

too many things aren't what they are
like most of us
                we dress in costumes
pose
     unhappy with our time
i never could dance like Fred Astaire or Ginger

o music music
there is the mind
a line of thot's its own litany
sung slightly out of tune
i know the imperfections in my voice
know choice is a matter of emotions
commitment to a place & time
the active present of the writing

1962   Vancouver
25 of us in the rain
protested the Bay of Pigs invasion

1963   Port Coquitlam
teaching a grade 4 class
heard
         over the intercom
of Kennedy's assassination
                         & cried

the contradictions are there in a lifetime
literature is no guarantee of a common good
i want a firmer ground to stand on

you do the best you can
as i saw that day the foal was born
you start with what's local
stands next to you
                    & move out
increase your range as your skill grows
& what's around you's taken care of

the w hat's low call
echoes thru these pages
lo cal or (i.e.)
                 what's immediate is
the word in front of me
the one beyond that that i'm reaching for
no muse at all really
simply this canadian foot
following a tentative line   forward
taking the time to tell you everything

the muse is western (greek)
the japanese saw poetry as everyman's
like thot or breathing
ambiguity was precisely what they wanted

it's social then
a point of view
political
the duty of a citizen
'a man betrays himself in his speech'

((why do they always question content, you
speak of form to counterbalance the question, they never ask what you believe in)
purpose can become conceit, shift beneath
the feet, the line of speech that's called
political, the signified slides below the sig-
nifier, gets lost in what's expedient, the
strength of english, its ambiguity, turned
against it, corrupted, the masked language
of law & politics, so distorted we empower
experts to interpret it)

in the distance clouds break
i'm sitting on the curb
crossing out words
resisting the urge to apologize

i am thinking it is better left behind
this city they no longer had a use for
make my way thru the shifting streets
along these sheets of paper to an ending

it is not over

it is never over

there is 'a third difficulty
with the usual definitions of parts of speech

they neglect form for meaning
although it is precisely through the *form* of our words and sentences
that we communicate our meanings.'
(James Sledd
A SHORT INTRODUCTION TO ENGLISH GRAMMAR)

& me
what am i doing
'building up a bracketing of asides'
standing here
outside the limits of this empty city
studying the cloud range
the shapes that shift
because it is the nature
of paper i have scribbled one word on
to shift it
            back & forth in my mind &
begin again
that way
among the tensions
the interplay between the letters
is to start at m
& then the a
leads thru to y
some questions answered
but the rest remain

not in the saints' names
which was beginnings
but in that space between
the s & t
among the shift of what at first seems arbitrary
'to go beyond the point where it is even neces-
            /sary to think in terms of words'
there
      which is t & here
more pain than we can bear
is bearable

M	Books I to III
A	which is begun
	& leads

                        on

                        that's all i'll say

january to december 1975

Statements
by the Poets

Robert Kroetsch: Seed Catalogue

What has come to interest me right now is what I suppose you can call the dream of origins. Obviously in the prairies, the small town and the farm are not merely places, they are remembered places. When they were the actuality of our lives, we had realistic fiction, and we had almost no poetry at all. Now in this dream condition, as dream-time fuses into the kind of narrative we call myth, we change the nature of the novel. And we start, with a new and terrible energy, to write the poems of the imagined real place.

I don't know when I began my continuing poem. It was years ago that my Aunt Mary O'Connor, one afternoon at her house in Edmonton, handed me the ledger that had been kept by her father, my grandfather, at a watermill in Bruce County, Ontario. Up until then I'd had no idea that my grandfather and Aunt Mary and I were in complicity. I finished the poem, their poem of the ledger, and called it *The Ledger*. But their poem demanded mine of me. And one afternoon in Calgary, in the Glenbow Archives (in the old building, not the spanking new one), in the basement, I stumbled upon an old seed catalogue. I wrote the poem called 'Seed Catalogue'. The two poems spoke to each other. They changed each other. I saw what was happening. We must always go back to the shore. I wrote, 'How I Joined the Seal Herd'. But the new poem created a new silence. In a huge Victorian house in upstate New York, in a room overlooking the Susquahanna river (the same river on whose banks Coleridge and Southey planned to establish their Pantisocracy), I wrote 'The Sad Phoenician'.

The continuing poem: not the having written, but the *writing*. The poem as long as a life. The lifelost poem.

The poem as big as a continent. Roy Kiyooka's *Transcanada Letters*. (How do you like *them* apples, Roy?)

And speaking of silence: see Phyllis Webb's 'Naked Poems'. It'll give you the shivers. The heebie-jeebies. Love is like.

See David Jones' *The Anathemata*. I go on coming back to that book. Trying to read the poem. A curse, so much like heaven.

And maybe *Blown Figures,* by Audrey Thomas, is a long poem disguised as a novel. The (at)venturing [in]to Africa. To neverywhere. Shore enough.

The writing the writing the writing. Fundamentally, I mean. The having written excludes the reader. We are left with our selves

as critics. We want to be readers. The continuing poem makes us

readers.

Homer's *The Odyssey,* forever being translated into new versions of the poem. How to do that without changing languages.

The self, returning from the self. Look out. Lookout.

Do not feed the apocalypse. Metamorphoses please.

Maybe the long poem replaces the old kitchen cabinet.

The seed catalogue is a shared book in our society. We have few literary texts approaching that condition. I wanted to write a poetic equivalent to the 'speech' of a seed catalogue. The way we read the page and hear its implications. Spring. The plowing, the digging, of the garden. The mapping of the blank, cool earth. The exact placing of the explosive seed.

Biography

Born and raised, as they say, in Alberta. Graduated from the University of Alberta in 1948 and went into the bush for six years, the Mackenzie River valley, Labrador. Came out and went to graduate school in the States. Went to Binghamton, New York, as a professor at the State University of New York; became co-editor of *boundary 2.* Stayed in New York State 17 years and wrote 6 novels, including *The Studhorse Man, Badlands, What the Crow Said.* Moved to the University of Manitoba in 1978. Moved to the University of Calgary in 1979.

Robert Kroetsch first began to write poetry when in his mid-thirties. His long poems constitute parts of a longer poem with the tentative title, *Field Notes.*

By Robert Kroetsch

The Stone Hammer Poems. Lantzville, British Columbia: Oolichan Books, 1st ed. 1975; 2nd ed. 1976.

The Ledger. London, Ont.: Applegarth Follies, 1975; Ilderton, Ontario: Brick/Nairn, 1979.

Seed Catalogue. Winnipeg: Turnstone Press, 1977.

The Sad Phoenician. Toronto: The Coach House Press, 1979.

Essays and Interviews

Brown, Russell M., 'An Interview with Robert Kroetsch', *University of Windsor Review,* Vol 7, No. 2 (Spring, 1972), pp. 1-8.

Cooley, Dennis and Robert Enright, 'Uncovering our Dream World: An Interview with Robert Kroetsch', *Arts Manitoba,* Vol 1, No. 1 (January/February, 1977), pp. 32-39.

Lecker, Robert, 'An Annotated Bibliography of Works by and about Robert Kroetsch', *Essays on Canadian Writing,* Numbers 7/8 (Fall, 1977), pp. 74-96.

Lecker, Robert, 'Robert Kroetsch's Poetry', *Open Letter,* Third Series, Number 8 (Spring, 1978), pp. 72-88.

Mandel, Ann, 'Uninventing Structures: Cultural Criticism and the Novels of Robert Kroetsch', *Open Letter,* Third Series, Number 8 (Spring, 1978), pp. 52-71.

Thomas, Peter, 'How Much Story Can a Song Take?' *The Fiddlehead,* No. 117 (Spring, 1978), pp. 108-117.

Thomas, Peter, '*The Ledger*: A Review', *The Fiddlehead,* No. 108 (Winter, 1976), pp. 114-117.

Wood, Susan, 'Reinventing the Word: Kroetsch's Poetry', *Canadian Literature,* No. 77 (Summer, 1978), pp. 28-39.

Stuart MacKinnon: The Intervals

My first attempts at writing in longer forms had something to do with the shape a figure makes as it moves in time, its configuration, so that by the time I came to write *The Intervals*, this concept was in place and actively shaping how I would approach the work. I believe I can trace the idea back to my reading of Gamow and Whitehead, and to Sir Thomas Browne's *The Garden of Cyrus*, and a book called *Blake and Yeats, the Contrary Vision*, by Hazard Adams. I wished to avoid the temporal narrative of simple cause-effect logic, so I tried to write discrete pieces that would go together as a longer work, trailing bits of themselves into each other and harking back, not by repeating actual lines as in a chorus, but serially, as in visual puns. Hark back not like going back to an earlier time, but as if history were something carried forward, or cyclic with a twist in the end which is the spiral forward.

The setting of the poem is a public park in Kingston, by the lakeshore, between the Hospital and the Kingston Penitentiary. The park was at that time under siege by the civic authorities who wanted to expropriate. The place worked its way into my consciousness until it became the central metaphor of the interval, which could expand and contract, taking moods, incidents and people into its structure. Kingston is a prime example of the 'garrison' town. The park presented an aspect of calm outlet to the lake, as an escape for the psyche locked behind walls in order to defend the civility of home and town against savage depredations from outside.

In 1971 I sat down with various fragments of earlier attempts and spent most of a year writing at a poem which was rewritten and trimmed down to what is printed here. It seems to me now, eight years later, that the state referred to as the interval works technically as a sculptural effect, moving through and around, sometimes calmly observing, sometimes passionately involved, moving between forces that pull and distort the eyes, bend the light. I think there is a parallel to my own background in the Eastern Townships of Quebec, being minority ghetto English within a majority French population, itself a minority nation within the larger Anglo nation, Canada, like a space station poised between gravitational fields of earth and sun.

As I got farther into the poem, certain developments suggested a resolution to the initial process of static conflict. Thus Heraclitos is chosen over Plato, dialectics over idealism, and political action over passive contemplation. This is not to say that I think the poem wants you to believe that if the big share of our taxes now going to intensive care and maximum security were to be diverted to community centres, all crime and sickness would vanish. But I do hope the poem suggests that state power is aligned with class interests and bureaucracy, so that social energy is diverted from corrective democratic creations into self-destructive social behaviour. I hope the poem suggests that, it was meant to.

By Stuart MacKinnon
The Welder's Arc. Kingston, Ont.: Quarry Press, 1969.
Skydeck. Ottawa: Oberon Press, 1971.
The Intervals. Toronto: The Coach House Press, 1974.
The Lost Surveyor. Ottawa: Oberon Press, 1976.
Mazinaw (forthcoming.)
ANTHOLOGY INCLUSIONS:
Made in Canada (Oberon Press)
A Strange Glory (McClelland and Stewart)
Boundary II (ed. M. Atwood)
RECORDINGS:
Four Kingston Poets (Kingston: Quarry Records)

Daphne Marlatt: Long as in Time? Steveston

I didn't set out to write a long poem so much as explore the place Steveston through a lengthening line. Hearing it push time – that came first.

I suppose, looking back on it, the lengthening line & the long poem were wound together. The line had to do with taking a deep breath – deep enough to in-spire a world, that is, giving back out what I took in. The world I live in, give & take, that permeable membrane I & my world are (one), operant in language. Steveston was a world very different from the one I usually inhabit, so I stood curiously to it. But even the word *inspire* with its odd reversability has meant both a breathing upon or into (outward) & a breathing in (inward), whether it's us or the world so interpenetrated we call it inspiration, having long since dropped the divine.

A spring day like this, Steveston, its soft rain & things sprouting & the smell of sea & soil on the wind. A future on the wind, time opening into a summer of growth, of heat, of long days of light & fish. Time & breath. Time for a deep breath. Time to be.

And it is just there, it seems, the long poem takes on time, proposes an open future as it embraces a closed past, successive, linear; how we got to here which is the door facing two ways. I prowled the docks, watching the fishermen getting ready to sail away. I paced the river, watching it rush toward an ocean where it would disappear. I learned the history of that place but its future remains, with some effort, open. In the deepest sense of it I wrote to be, I wrote for Steveston to be, here now & myself here now in it. The world I was writing was & is a world I in the company of everyone could continue to live in: creation, goes on being created as writing enacts it. But because we have got to where we have out of our common history, each of us writes in the teeth of a likelihood of closed time, an end of 'our' own making yes, but also an end beyond our individual volition & creation. That likelihood surfaced in the poem not because the poem is a complete, if closed, system, but because it opens to the future, keeps pace with the river. Because we do, exactly, read in a line from left to right &

down the page, the long poem unfolds in time, sequentially, as we imagine our lives do. Yet we experience ourselves in the shape of our lives. Before writing *Steveston*, I listened to life stories there & the man or woman I saw at the end of each story was very much the shape of it – both the result & shaper of, in the telling. They each of them lived or had lived beside a river rushing ineluctably toward the sea, but that river never stopped & never stops coming tho our lives propose that time does.

The narrative of a long poem isn't necessarily linear, tho it may go on for many pages. I think of *Steveston* as actually a movement around, based on return. A cycle of poems, it moves around & keeps returning to the central interface of human lives with the river, picking up the threads (roads) that lead there. My image for it was a network, the ways in which all of the poems & all of a poem's parts, as all of us & where we live, are interconnected. The cycle tells as many of those knots of connection as it can. It used other people's speech, other voices my own moves with & against. It moves around & around its own end where the river disappears, & it ends when it can go no further, where it dives back in to the heart of things.

I've been talking about *Steveston* as writing because that was what I was engaged in. But the context of the writing was that it was half of a collaboration, the other half being Robert Minden's photographs. We worked separately together: that is, we often drove down together to Steveston, then separated to encounter the place & its people on our own terms, he with his camera & me with my notebook. Sometimes we met people together & sometimes one of us would bring the other to meet someone we had encountered previously. We exchanged our experience at every point, although I found it difficult to convey to him the fullness of what I was sensing other than in the written piece that finally completed a day, even days later. He would talk about his meetings with the people he photographed & the way he was photographing, often in great detail, but similarly I didn't 'see' what he was getting at until, days or weeks later, I saw the prints.

What the camera sees & what the word says are both aspects of a vision that is larger than either or even both of us because it is a vision on that interpenetration of us & the world Steveston came to be for us, with its people, its streets, its docks & river & earth spaces – particulars each of us, ourselves particular, came to meet.

Biography

Born in Australia, 1942. Immigrated from Malaysia to Vancouver, 1951. Went to school, UBC & Indiana. Worked as cashier, clerk, waitress, secretary. Married, one child, divorced. Taught English at community colleges in California & Vancouver. Collected & edited oral histories for the Provincial Archives. Poetry editor for *The Capilano Review* 1973-76. Now edits the prose magazine *periodics* with Paul de Barros. Continues to live in Vancouver.

By Daphne Marlatt

Frames of a Story. Toronto: Ryerson Press, 1968.
leaf leaf/s. Los Angeles: Black Sparrow Press, 1969.
Rings. Vancouver Community Press, 1971.
Vancouver Poems. Toronto: The Coach House Press, 1972.
Steveston. Vancouver: Talonbooks, 1974.
Our Lives. Carrboro, NC: Truck Press, 1975.
    Canadian edition to be released from Oolichan Press 1979.
Zócalo. Toronto: Coach House Press, 1977.
The Story, She Said. Vancouver: B.C. Monthly Press, 1977.
EDITOR:
Steveston Recollected: A Japanese-Canadian History.
    Victoria: Provincial Archives of British Columbia, 1975.
Opening Doors (with Carole Itter). Provincial Archives of
    British Columbia, 1979.

Reviews of 'Steveston'

Baldwin, Neil, *Small Press Review,* No. 29/30
(June/July, 1975).

Barbour, Douglas, 'The Phenomenological I: Daphne Marlatt's
Steveston,' in *Figures in a Ground: Canadian Essays on
Modern Literature Collected in Honor of Sheila Watson,* ed.
Diane Bessai, David Jackel (Saskatoon: Western Producer
Prairie Books, 1978).

Lecker, Robert A., *Quill & Quire* (April, 1975).

Lecker, Robert A., 'Daphne Marlatt's Poetry', in *Canadian
Literature* (Autumn 1978), pp. 56-67.

Lillard, Charles, *The Malahat Review* No. 38 (April, 1976),
pp. 144-150.

Newton, Stuart, *West Coast Review* No. 9-10, pp. 67-68.

Novik, Mary, *Vancouver Sun* (Friday, October 31, 1975).

Perry, Art, *The Province* (February 28, 1975).

Woodcock, George, 'Beyond the Divide, Part II',
Georgia Straight (Oct 16-23, 1975), p. 6.

Interviews:

Arnason, David, Dennis Cooley, and Robert Enright,
'There's this and this connexion' in *CVII,* III, 1 (Spring 1977),
pp. 28-33.

Bowering, George, 'Keep Witnessing', in *Open Letter* III, 2
(Fall 1975), pp. 26-38.

Bowering, George, 'Given This Body' in *Open Letter* IV, 3
(Spring, 1979), pp. 32-88.

Kemp (Chalmers), Penny, 'Circumlocutions', in *Journal of
Canadian Poetry* I, 1 (Winter '78), pp. 71-76.

Reviews of Other Books:

Bowering, George, review of *Vancouver Poems* in 'Lines on the
Grid', *Open Letter* II, 8 (Summer 1974), pp. 94-99.

Coleman, Victor, review of *Rings* in *Open Letter* II, 1,
pp. 78-80.

Davey, Frank, 'Daphne Marlatt' in *From There to Here:
A Guide to English-Canadian Literature Since 1960*
(Erin: Press Porcepic, 1974), pp. 193-197.

Dawson, Fielding, 'A Psychic Hammer' in *Open Letter* III, 7 (Summer 1977), pp. 108-110, on *Our Lives*.

Mays, John Bentley, 'Ariadne: Prolegomenon to the Poetry of Daphne Marlatt', in *Open Letter* III, 3 (Fall, 1975), pp. 5-33, on *Vancouver Poems*.

Steward, D.E., review of *Zócalo* in *San Francisco Review of Books*, IV, 1 (May 1978), p. 17.

Varney, Ed, review of *Vancouver Poems* in *West Coast Review* No. 9-10, pp. 72-73.

Don McKay: Long Sault

The long poem is imaginative space in which a person knows
he has room to stretch his muscles and time for meditation,
travel, metamorphosis, loitering. A.R. Ammons got attracted
by a roll of adding-machine tape in a store and wound up
writing a long thin poem on it; another person buys an empty
house because he can feel the kind of music that will happen in
its rooms.

But some subjects demand that length, especially in Canada,
where there's a strong tug on our minds from the unknown,
and poems can get pulled out like tape measures and/or fishing
line. *Long Sault* began with the subject, which I'd carried
around a long time and needed to write – a big energy and loss,
both for myself and the community. When the hydroelectric
dam was constructed at Cornwall, Ontario during the late
fifties, the St. Lawrence River flooded upstream as far as
Iroquois, submerging a length of shoreline rich in history and
tradition. Villages like Wales, Mille Roches, Moulinette,
Dickinson's Landing were 'relocated', and – focal point of this
poem – the Long Sault Rapids was drowned. It was only after
I got going that I found myself in a longer sequence which then
grew by grope and feel. At first I had in mind something short
and tough, left jab, angry elegy. But doing that I found other
planes of the subject, realized that the moves and power of the
long sault weren't really locked up in the dam, began thinking
of all the rapids I'd experienced and found them moving in
surprising places and pushing the writing into different forms,
looked into historical accounts which touched on the long
sault, like those by Alexander Henry and George Heriot (whose
words introduce 'At the Long Sault Parkway'), and I guess gen-
erally got sucked in, the way my eyes always got sucked into
watching the long sault during Sunday excursions, and still get
mesmerized by that furious stillness.

By Don McKay

Air Occupies Space (poems). Windsor: Sesame Press, 1973.
Long Sault. London: Applegarth Follies, 1975.
Lependu (long poem, concerning the hanged man).
   London, Ont.: Nairn Press, 1978.
October Edge (poems, in press).

Robin Blaser The Moth Poem

The Moth Poem is one section of a long unfinished work, *The Holy Forest,* and was written in 1964. One line of it indicates that I had begun to think of the new country which came to be Canada. It is a serial poem, according to the agreement Jack Spicer and I reached to name the kind of narrative we were working on around 1960. Robert Duncan, planning to write on the poetry of both of us in 1962, called it neo-narrative. For both Jack and me, poetry had fallen into time, like beauty itself, and attendant divinity. (Blakes's Los as the figuration of imaginative loss would come to mind in my later years to explain much to me of this argument with time.) The term serial was not adapted from serial music, but was intended to suggest the diremptions of belief, even in poetry, all around us. The broken, which is broken heart and broken mind, simulta-neously cultural and personal, was never simply personal. Jack was to call the poet a 'time mechanic.' And it fits. Models for such serial construction were found in Rilke's *Duino Elegies, Sonnets to Orpheus* and Robert Duncan's *Medieval Scenes.* Such poems deconstruct meanings and compose a wildness of meaning in which the I of the poet is not the centre but a returning and disappearing note.

The serial poem, then, gives special emphasis to time – poem following poem in sequence of the writing – often with one dominant musical note or image, such as the moth, which is the gift or the dictated. During the composition of *The Moth Poem,* moths were attendant – strangely, whenever, wherever, and noticed by others, about my head, on my shoulder, at my lamp. This is the issue of the opening poems. 'A Literalist' and 'The Literalist.' So, the poem begins with a moth caught in the strings of the piano – literally – it woke me with a marvelous, tentative music in the middle of the night. The beginning and a command. Thus, the exact, the literal, the dictated are keys to the poem: for example, one of the Atlantis poems depends upon my having knocked over a glass of water, which accident inundated everything on my study desk. The central event of the poem is the creation of the moth in 'it it it it,' as it hit the dark window. This appearance of the moth is preceded by 'Paradise Quotations', made entirely of lines from my reading that come to mind freely and wildly – Nijinsky's diary, Coleridge, Hawthorne, and the intertwining couplets of Erasmus Darwin – just before 'it' hit the window. The serial meaning ends in 'Salut', a greeting to appearing and disappearing things, guided by the fragment of H.D's priest, a wand against mediocrity. The musical notes closing the original text of *The Moth Poem* are Pythagoras' notation of the musical intervals between the planets, the oldest tradition of the music of the spheres – that is, according to Pliny, *Hist. Nat.*, II. Oddly heard.

Some time passed, the poem was published as a small book, the moths had returned to their secrets, when the exact events of the poem, 'The Translator', occured. The early morning, the bit of a dream of a pool, the Mexican coffee spoon staining the drainboard, the ashtray, the work on the translation from Catullus, the moth burrowed in the ashes – this final little poem, too late for the book, is a true ending in metrical openness and astonishment.

I think that serial narrative is useful to speak in time, close to the limit of what we are – god and man in terms of this century's questions. The poet is not the centre of meaning, and if he were, the horror would be his dearest subject. The serial poet chances it to think again as if everything had to be thought anew. Accepting time, he reaches the 'unnameable' (to borrow from Beckett), 'dances' there (to borrow from Yeats), and composes 'words, loves' (to borrow from Spicer). The serial poem is not simply a sequence. It is meant to be a narrative that transfigures time, our limit, mine. I have wanted to use the form because it makes language direct and insistent without reference to a grid of meaning, which in our time has become intolerable, a-historical, a lie. Delicate and harsh are the words that come to mind to describe this form. Since form is always the reach of content, rhythmical and musical, the serial structure has allowed me to imagine the indeterminate nature of what we are beyond finitude and other small dead ends.

What a trip to lay on *The Moth Poem!* It is a small poem full of grace notes. These notes are meant to suggest a fundamental purpose of serial narrative beyond one poem. From which one writes.

Biography
Born in Denver, Colorado, 1925. Canadian citizen 1972.

By Robin Blaser
The Moth Poem. San Francisco: Open Space, 1964.
Les Chimères. San Francisco: Open Space, 1964.
Cups. San Francisco: Four Seasons Foundation, 1968.
Image-Nations 1-12 & The Stadium of the Mirror. London: Ferry Press, 1974.
Image-Nations 13 & 14, Luck Unlock Oneluck, Sky-Stone, Suddenly, Gathering. Vancouver: Cobblestone Press, 1975.
EDITED:
The Collected Books of Jack Spicer. Los Angeles: Black Sparrow, 1975.
ESSAYS:
'The Fire', in Donald M. Allen and Warren Tallman, eds., *The Poetics of the New American Poetry* (N.Y.: Grove Press, 1974).
'The Practice of Outside', in *The Collected Books of Jack Spicer* (Los Angeles: Black Sparrow, 1975).
'The Stadium of the Mirror', in *Image-Nations* 1-12 above.
'Mary Butts, 1893-1937', afterword to a new edition of her *Imaginary Letters* (Vancouver: Talon Books, 1979).
IN PROCESS:
The complete, *The Holy Forest,* a collection of poems begun in 1960, a long narrative. And two prose works of freed prose, *Astonishments* and *Death-Work* with Dennis Wheeler. *Astonishments* is an autobiography of poetry and *Death-Work* is a dialogue with Dennis Wheeler until he died of leukemia. Dennis Wheeler was one of my companions of imagination, Jack Spicer, Charles Olson and Dennis Wheeler.

Am editing Jack Spicer's play, *Troilus.* Also currently at work on the selected poems of George Bowering with an essay on what I see therein.

Frank Davey: King of Swords

The King of Swords always struck me as the most secular
figure in the Tarot pack – the furthest from earth and the most
committed to power. I was putting the *L'An Trentiesme* collection together for Stan Persky in 1971 when I came across the
MS. of a set of poems I'd written ten years earlier 'in response'
(I'd thought) to Malory's *The Book of Arthur*. They'd been published in *Tish 14*. There was something fundamentally
unrealized and unsavoury about them – they were heavy-
handed, mechanical, gloomy. I found myself increasingly more
preoccupied with them than with the Persky collection, and
with the new connections to my first marriage, to the Tarot
pack, to contemporary event. Most of my serial poems are
records, almost transcripts, of profound preoccupation. *King of
Swords* was written in about a two-week period, in a sequence
very close to the published one, five or six of its sections being
written at a time at nights between midnight and two, at least
two sections being written concurrently in a twenty-minute
span. It was a record of accumulating insight, done with a
conscious committment to preserving the emotion of discovery. I wanted the 'story' of the poem's writing to be as present in
the text as any other story – Guenevere's, the Great Lakes',
Biafra's, my own. For it was in this story that the life of the
poem moved, that life through which all its characters, particularly Arthur, Guenevere, Lancelot, and the Tarot figures,
could speak as the reader's contemporaries. This is a major
insistence of the poem: that all its elements whether
Arthurian, American, or personal are happening on the day of
the poem's writing. None of these elements to me were allu-
sional, historical, or even archetypal – they were intrinsic to
the phenomenological now.

Biography
Frank Davey was born in Vancouver, B.C., in 1940, but moved
with his family to the farming village of Abbotsford shortly
thereafter. He attended the University of British Columbia
from 1957-63 (BA 1961, MA 1963), where he was one of the

founding editors of *Tish* magazine and submitted the first
creative writing MA thesis at the university. He has taught
at Royal Roads Military College in Victoria, B.C. (1963-1969)
and at York University (since 1970) where he was the first
coordinator of the York creative writing program. He was
Writer-in-Residence at Sir George Williams University in
1969-70. He held Canada Council fellowships in 1965-66 and
1974-75.

Since the founding of *Tish* in 1961, he has been exceedingly
active as an editor and critic. He founded the important journal
of contemporary research and criticism, *Open Letter*, in 1965.
He published a study of Charles Olson in 1970, a study of Earle
Birney in 1971, a guide to Canadian literature since 1960 (*From
There to Here*, Press Porcepic) in 1974, and has a study of Louis
Dudek and Raymond Souster in press. He is an editor of The
Coach House Press, co-editor of the Coach House Quebec
Translations series, and general editor of the Talonbooks New
Canadian Criticism series.

By Frank Davey

D-Day and After. Vancouver: Tishbooks, 1962.
City of the Gulls and Sea. Victoria: 1964.
Bridge Force. Toronto: Contact Press, 1965.
The Scarred Hull. Calgary: Imago, 1966.
Four Myths for Sam Perry. Vancouver: Talonbooks, 1970.
Weeds. Toronto: The Coach House Press, 1970.
Griffon. Toronto: Massasauga Editions, 1972.
King of Swords. Vancouver: Talonbooks, 1972.
l'An Trentiesme: Selected Poems 1961-1970.
    Vancouver: Vancouver Community Press, 1972.
Arcana. Toronto: The Coach House Press, 1973.
The Clallam. Vancouver: Talonbooks, 1973.
War Poems. Toronto: Coach House Press MS. Editions, 1979.
Selected Poems, ed. Michael André. Vancouver: Talonbooks,
    in press.

Articles about Frank Davey

Andre, Michael. Review of *Arcana, Queen's Quarterly* 80
    (Winter 1973), pp. 658-659.

Barbour, Douglas. 'Frank Davey: Finding Your Voice: to Say What Must Be Said: The Recent Poetry,' in Jack David, ed., *Brave New Wave* (Windsor: Black Moss Press, 1979), pp. 65-82.

Bowering, George. 'Starting at our skins' (interview), *Open Letter*, Fourth Series, no. 3 (Spring 1979), pp. 89-181.

Komisar, Elizabeth. 'Frank Davey' (Interview), *White Pelican* (1975), pp. 49-58.

Komisar, Elizabeth. 'Frank Davey,' in C.H. Gervais, ed. *The Writing Life* (Windsor: Black Moss Press, 1976), pp. 179-192.

Mays, John Bentley. 'About Frank Davey,' *White Pelican* (1975), pp. 59-61.

George Bowering: Look into your Ear & Write: Allophanes

For years I wrote scads of short Canadian lyrics, quick takes learned from the Imagists, glances outward at the world. In that way I learned how to speak. It was a necessary (you might call it:) apprenticeship.

After you have spent a decade learning to speak, you might be tempted to speak out on everything, again & again. In Canada we have some duffers who do that, all right.

So I reacht a point where I didnt bother remarking what others are here to remark — dead dogs or bothersome lovers. I got into the practice of listening, for meditations. All my long poems are meditations.

On the BC Ferry, David McFadden closes his eyes & meditates. In this attitude he hears all the people's voices around him. David is picking up the news & views of the world. He is a good listener.

I cock my ear. What I want to hear is the voice that enters my secluded study. I dont care, really, to enquire of it where it is coming from. If it is loud enough it is all round one. In this manner I settle the perennial question put to poets: what is your concept of an audience? I am aware of myself as audience. When one plays by ear, it is not to hear what one is putting out. There is enough to do in catching what comes in.

As I get older, I come more to realize that my activity as a poet composing is an extension of my desirous childhood Christianity. I want like crazy to get here alone & hear God's voice. I mean it. If I hear the gods instead, I am acknowledging, like it or not, my adulthood.

This poem was written from September to December in 1974, & from all appearances seems to bridge a gap between the politics of *At War with the* U.S. & the cultural narrative of *A Short Sad Book.*

It began with a sentence heard in the author's head: The snowball appears in Hell every morning at seven. It was said in the voice of Jack Spicer.

The author knew something was up, & went deliberately to hear some more voices as best he could, & hurried to write

[Gr. allos, other + Gr. phanein, to appear]

down what they were saying. Astute readers will recognize some of them.

Allo means all. Phanes means appearances. The poem tries not to get one without the other. The scientific usage of the term attends the shifting colours of mineral formations, such as stalactites, lights in a cave.

The word could also be translated as those things which are other than what they at first appear to be, all taken together.

By or about George Bowering

Author of many books of poetry, including *Rocky Mountain Foot* (1969), *Touch (Selected Poems)* (1971), *In The Flesh* (1973), and *The Catch* (1976), all from McClelland and Stewart.

Also author of several books of fiction, including *Mirror on the Floor* (1967), *Autobiology* (1972), *Flycatcher and other Stories* (1974), *A Short Sad Book* (1977), *Protective Footwear* (1978).

He is also an essayist, playwright, and editor. One of the founding editors of the notorious west coast poetry journal, *Tish*, he went on to edit a magazine of longer poems, *Imago*, as well as a series of literary monographs called *Beaver Kosmos Folios*.

His most characteristic work explores areas of writing that would be difficult to designate as either verse or prose. They are usually called 'Serial Poems' & published as separate books. These would include *Curious* (1974), *Geneve* (1970), and *Allophanes* (1977).

He received a Governor-General's award in poetry for the 1969 volumes, *The Gangs of Kosmos* and *Rocky Mountain Foot*.

He has received two Canada Council Awards, in 1971 and 1977.

He was Writer-in-Residence at Sir George Williams University in 1967-68.

He has taught American and Canadian literature at several universities, most recently Simon Fraser University on the west coast. He is currently working on a novel and a book about recent Canadian fiction.

'The Poetry of George Bowering' by Ken Norris, in *Brave New Wave*, ed. Jack David, (Windsor: Black Moss, 1979).

Interview in *Out-Posts* by Caroline Bayard & Jack David, (Erin, Ont.: Press Porcepic, 1978).

Interview 'Curioser and Curioser' by Marianne Lafon and Ken Norris in *Cross Country* 5, reprinted in *Western Windows* (Vancouver: Comm Cept Press, 1977).

Interview in next issue of *The Capilano Review*, by David McFadden, Paul de Barros, Sharon Thiessen, and Bill Shermbrucker.

'George Bowering' in Frank Davey, *From There to Here* (Erin, Ont.: Press Porcépic, 1974), pp. 57-62.

'Introduction' by Robin Blaser in Bowering's *Selected Poems* (Vancouver: Talonbooks, in press).

Roy Kiyooka: The Fontainebleau Dream Machine

After-thoughts concerning a long pome in 18 frames titled the F.D.M.

re-turning, this time, – in the guise of A Child of Literature: 'I' am standing on my tip-toes to buy a ticket for a ride on the fabled *The Fontainebleau Dream Machine* clutching the guard rail around the windy loading platform, my heart heaves as it slowly descends. etcetera. 'imagine' my consternation, my terror, when i discovered that the higher it went the more the earth became a tiny speck and all around – there was nothing, nothing but a piercing, wind-borne outcry. the F.D.M. incurs, within the body of its own forebodings, the notion that Language-as-Rhetorick is, itself, a terrifying dream. the F.D.M. is, among other things, my oftimes bemused Homage to the whole domain of European Art, which, together with Christianity & its twin, Capitalism – I am an errant child, an orphan of. the F.D.M. embodies a Quest for the true body, the abode, of one man's Dialect among a host of, oftimes, alien ikons. the text & its co-equal, the illustrations, propose the pleasure of moving in among light-struck runes. the slowly turning propeller of our adamant History proposes that the yet-to-be-written Canadian Epic will be a wind-borne series of discrete images, 4000 lines long, with an ocean at either end for ballast. everytime I re-read the F.D.M.... I re-invent myself. 'it' is a musical score for a small ensemble. a window, sky-light an open door.

By Roy Kiyooka
Things, of divers consequences, viz. *Biography:* enfolded in A BIBLIOGRAPHY- BIOLOGY OF, ONE MAN'S MIND-GRAFFITI ON THE WALLS OF... With a heaping-up of Chronology in, the underlined titles. Everyword, written, spoken, thought, or dreamt, re-affirms the doubts concerning the actual whereabouts of 'the author', who, like the proverbial lover, disappeared into the aura of his indiscretions. Everytime he is asked for his biography – he takes another inventory of his several selves. A man & his words, however paltry, rise daily

into the same phenomenological world. 'Art is A Calling. A
Fool &. A Scold: An actual s-p-e-a-k-i-n-g — o-u-t-

A BIBLIOGRAPHY-BIOLOGY OF ONE MAN'S MIND-GRAFFITI
ON THE WALLS OF...
Kyoto Airs. Vancouver: Periwinkle Press, 1964.
4th Avenue Pomes in *Imago* II, (Vancouver: 1965).
12 Collages & a pome, for G.B.'s *The Man in Yellow Boots*
    (Mexico City: El Corno Emplumado, 1965).
4 (xerox) illustrations, plus Cover, for Dorothy Livesay's *The*
    Unquiet Bed (Toronto: Ryerson Press, 1967).
Nevertheless These Eyes. Toronto: The Coach House Press,
    1967.
Stonedgloves, with photos by the author. Toronto: The Coach
    House Press, 1970.
Eye in the Landscape, a 40 page photo sequence. 1 of 15 books
    comprising the B.C. Almanac (NFB Stills Division, 1970).
Cover, & pomes for *Canadian Art Today* issue of *Studio*
    International, 1970.
Two Interviews & asst. Letters, *White Pelican* (Winter 1971).
Group of seven letters to Anne Brodzky, *artscanada*
    (Feb/March, 1972).
Stonedfootwear photos in *White Pelican* (Winter, 1973).
artscanadaafloat with G. Gilbert, Carole Itter, & Krisy van
    Eyck. *B.C. Monthly,* edited by G.G., 1974.
A Section from *7 Day Backcountry Trip,* (*Imago* 20, 1974).
Kiyooka: 25 Years (Vancouver Art Gallery Catalogue).
    Talonbooks, 1975.
Transcanadaletter (Letters, Biography, Narrative). Vancouver:
    Talonbooks, 1975.
Mutualities (Roy Kiyooka, Richard Turner). *Vanguard,* Oct. 77,
    Vol. 6, No 7.
Fontainebleau Dream Machine Texts & Illustrations.
    Toronto: The Coach House Press, 1977.
Of Seasonal Pleasures & Small Hindrances, B.C. Monthly,
    1978.

13 Cameras / Vancouver, Vanguard, Nov. 78, Vol. 7, No. 8.

An Introduction, of sorts, to *13 Cameras,* plus 17 pages of photos, (*13 Cameras / Vancouver,* Brock Webber Printers, 1979.

Kiyooka: Born in Moose Jaw, by Wilfred Watson, *NeWest Review* Vol. 1 No. 11, May '76, p. 5 ff.

Roy Kiyooka's Poetry (an appreciation), by George Bowering in *Kiyooka, 25 Years: Catalogue of a Retrospective Exhibition,* July '75.

IN PROCESS:

T.T. &) The Company He Keeps. withoutwords, a 250 page photo-novella.

Seasonal Salt/Tidings, a colour xerox (haiku) suite.

bpNichol: some words on the martyrology march 12 1979

everything is part of something else. somewhere in my 20s i
became conscious of certain threads, certain themes & less
specific contents that spread thru my work, thru my poetry,
its concerns. i began to think of this as one long work divided
(roughly) into two sections: *The Books of the Dead & The
Books of the Living.* I saw the *Books of the Dead* as being
comprised of *The Journey* (1962-63 – discarded), *Journeying &
The Returns* (1963-66 – published CHP 1967), *The Undiscovered Country* (written 66-67 & worked at till 71 or so when i
discarded it), *Scraptures* (1965 to 69 – published in various
sections in magazines & pamphlets) & *The Captain Poetry
Poems* (1965 to 1968 – published by Blewointment 1971).
The problem was i couldn't make it work. *The Journey & The
Undiscovered Country* failed because i had not yet grasped the
full principle of the utanikki, the poetic diary, & as a result i
romanticized my experience to a disgusting degree. I temporarily abandoned this notion and began work on *The Martyrology.* along the way two other linked works appeared: *Mono
Tones* (1967-69 – published by Talonbooks 1971) & *The Plun-
kett Papers* (1969-71 – discarded for the same reasons as *The
Journey* et al). still i pushed aside the notion of the larger work,
tho i was aware of the links, & continued working on *The
Martyrology.*
      The text included in this anthology – Book IV of *The
Martyrology* – began after a long period of silence (approxi-
mately two years chronologically (February 73 to January 75)
but much longer subjectively – & hence the Merwin quote at
the beginning:

Looking for it all over the place
three years
carrying it all the time like a baby

a period in which i thot *The Martyrology* had perhaps finished
itself. Then the line 'purpose is a porpoise' came & from that
strange beginning the poem itself began to unwind.

The echo, of course, was a Bissett quote in 'a funny name for claimd similur creaturs / one a porpoise / th othur a dolphin', a quote which reverbrated for me with the similarities & differences between Bill's work & my own. It began (& begins) too with a statement of my poetic goal:

the precision of openness
is not a vagueness
it is an accumulation
cumulous

Thus the Clouds section (which follows The Book of Common Prayer in Book II) was re-invoked at the same time as a statement of my retroactively recognized formal model (the utanikki) was restated – opening the self as wide as possible while struggling for precision thru a meditational process of accumulation. Since the Clouds section was also the one which outlined the history of the saints' migration to earth, 'left the white streets of that higher town / to tumble down the long blue highway to the trees' / tops', i was led back gradually thru a preoccupation with surface, & the depth implicit in it, to the 'A / B / ginning / of the town / the saints came down from'. And i was led too to draw back certain veils that had lain across my sense of language, (ca. 1967 in *postcard between* – 'vague // like the clouds // my language was'), precisely because i was 'down at the surface where the depth is', reading words as single sentences in which messages lay. At the same time the pun's strength (auditory, as in 'purpose' & 'porpoise', or visual, as in 'the M / the ME / the s is / a way of starting') was utilized far more than in any previous book. These accumulating energy points thrust me thru Book IV in one year, the poem being written as one long continuous take, a formal evolution from Books I, II & III and leading on into the chains of the forthcoming final book of *The Martyrology*, Book V. *The Martyrology* spans 12 years of my writing (1967 to 1979). With *Book V* behind me, as far as the journal writing aspects, i found the notion of the *Books of the Dead & Living* returning, gaining focus precisely because *The Martyrology* seemed finished but some larger vision seemed barely begun.

What is a long poem? perhaps it is simply a long life or some trust in the durational aspect of being alive. it's a tremendous leap of faith to even start one, to even think 'hey i'll be alive long enough that this form seems the best way to say what i have to say'. certainly some faith in process pushes me on knowing even as i do so that the question of audience, who precisely the poem is intended for, is an interesting & unresolved one. as the work continues i actually feel i may have finally begun *The Books of the Living,* have written myself far enough to the other side of my childhood as a writer, as a human being, out of my past, out of the dead days into at least a present that is life & from which my perspective, my contents, can change. this was my perception in the mid-60s, that i would reach a point where my concerns, such as they were, would undergo a shift, but that the books that came before (the ones i then had yet to write) were the absolute soil out of which those (these in this case) would come.

Where do those earlier works fit? That is the question that still troubles me. In a sense they are sub-texts to *The Martyrology,* and as such do not so much come before it as they do lie under it. I suppose an ideal reading would be one which begins with 1) *The Martyrology,* but then dips into *Journeying & The Returns, Scraptures* & *The Captain Poetry Poems* along the way, much as one might read earlier history to gain a better appreciation of a particular period. This is a notion only, a tentative map. I have begun a new work, *A Counting,* which continues on from Book v of *The Martyrology.* The first Book of the work, A Book of Hours, abandons the talk about language that so informed *The Martyrology* & moves outward into the concepts, people & places that have evolved in & around the writing. Lines that i wrote in the unpublished *May Day Book* in the spring of 1976 seem appropriate to this whole struggle:

'dying & being born & dying
 & being born & dying & being born'

Biography

Born in Vancouver in 1944. Made his early reputation thru publication in European little magazines in the mid-60's as part of the international concrete poetry movement & was included in numerous exhibitions & anthologies there & in North & South America. Since 1970 has performed as part of the Four Horsemen, a sound / performance / writing collective. Is co-founder of the Toronto Research Group, contributing editor to *Open Letter,* member of the editorial collectives for Coach House Press & Underwhich Editions, & was the editor from 1965 to 1978 of Ganglia Press (co-founded with David Aylward) which published *Ganglis, GrOnk & Synapses* magazines as well as numerous pamphlets. Subject of a movie *Sons of Captain Poetry* by poet / novelist / film-maker Michael Ondaatje & editor of the first collection of Canadian visual poetry *The Cosmic Chef* as well as co-editor, with Steve McCaffery, of a major book on sound poetry *Sound Poetry: A Catalogue.* Won the Governor General's award for poetry in 1970. Has issued one album of solo sound work *Motherlove,* an earlier extended play recording *Borders,* & most recently was one half of an EP with Sean O'Huigin & Ann Southam included in O'Huigin's *Poe Tree: A Simple Introduction To Experimental Poetry.* He has recorded two albums as part of the Four Horsemen: *Nada Canadada,* & *Live in the West.* Works in a wide variety of forms. Resident in Toronto since 1964 where he works as a theradramist with Therafields, an organization devoted to exploring a wide range of solutions to problems of emotional disturbance.

By bpNichol

a note on the form of things as currently perceived.
(August 15, 1979)
SCRAPTURES (THE BOOKS OF THE DEAD /
THE BOOKS OF THE LIVING)
SUB-TEXTS:
Journeying & the returns. Toronto: The Coach House Press,
1967.

Scraptures:
> *Basic Sequences.* Toronto: Massasauga Editions, 1974.
> *Second Sequence.* Toronto: Ganglia Press, 1965.
> *Third Sequence.* Toronto: Ganglia Press, 1966.
> *Fourth Sequence.* Niagara Falls, N.Y.: Press Today Niagara,
>   1966.
> *Tenth Sequence.* Toronto: Ganglia Press, 1967.
> *Eleventh Sequence.* Toronto: Fleye Press, 1967.

The Captain Poetry Poems. Vancouver: Blewointment Press,
    1971.

INTRODUCTORY TEXT:

Mono Tones. Vancouver: Talonbooks, 1971.

TEXTS:

The Martyrology Books I to IV. Toronto: The Coach House
    Press, 1972/1976.

The Martyrology Book V. Unpublished.

A Counting
> I: *A Book of Hours.* (In progress.)
> II: *Some Books of Journeying*
>   Vol 1. You Too, Nicky. (In progress.)

Further Reading of Long, Book-length or Serial Poems Suggested by the Poets and Editor

Ammons, A.R. *Tape for the Turn of the Year*. Ithaca, N.Y.: Cornell University Press, 1965.

Atwood, Margaret. *The Journals of Susannah Moodie*. Toronto: Oxford University Press, 1970.

———. *Power Politics*. Toronto: Oxford University Press, 1971.

Basho, Matsuo. *Back Roads to Far Towns*. Trans. by Corman and Susumu. New York: Grossman Publishers, 1968.

———. *The Narrow Road to the Deep North and Other Travel Sketches*. Trans. by Nobuyuki Yuasa. U.K.: Penquin, 1966.

Berrigan, Ted. *Sonnets*. N.Y.: Grove Press, 1967, c. 1964.

Birney, Earle. *Trial of a City*. Toronto: The Ryerson Press, 1952. Also in *The Collected Poems of Earle Birney* (Toronto: McClelland and Stewart, Ltd., 1975) as 'The Damnation of Vancouver.'

Bissett, Bill. *Lebanon Voices*. Toronto: Weed/Flower, 1967.

———. *Pomes for Yoshi*. Vancouver: Talonbooks, 1977.

Bunting, Basil. *Briggflatts*. London: Fulcrum, 1966.

Coleman, Victor. *America*. Toronto: The Coach House Press, 1972.

Dewdney, Christopher. *Golders Green*. Toronto: The Coach House Press, 1971.

———. *The Palaeozoic Geology of London, Ontario*. Toronto: The Coach House Press, 1973.

———. *Spring Trances in the Control Emerald Night*. California: Figures, 1978.

Doolittle, Hilda. *Trilogy*. N.Y.: New Directions, 1973.

Dorn, Edward. *Slinger*. Berkeley, Calif.: Wingbow, 1975.

Dudek, Louis. *Atlantis*. Montreal: Delta Canada, 1967.

———. *L'Europe*. Toronto: Laocoon (Contact) Press, 1954.

Duncan, Robert. 'Passages' in *Bending the Bow* (N.Y.: New Directions, 1968).

———. *Roots and Branches* N.Y.: Scribners, 1964.

———. 'Structures of Rime' in *The Opening of the Field* (N.Y.: Grove Press, 1960).

———. *Tribunals*. L.A.: Black Sparrow, 1970.

Dyck, E.F. *Odpoems Et*. Moose Jaw: Coteau Books, 1978.

Fawcett, Brian. *The Opening*. Vancouver: New Star Books, 1974.

Fencott, P.C. *The Legends of Jack O'Kent*. Toronto: Gronk, 1978.

Galway and Cinnell. *The Book of Nightmares*. N.Y.: Hougton Mifflin, 1971.

Geddes, Gary. *War and Other Measures*. Toronto: House of Anansi Press Ltd., 1976.

Gilbert, Gerry. *And*. Vancouver: Blewointment Press, 1971.

Gotlieb, Phyllis. *The Works*. Toronto: Calliope Press, 1978.

Griffiths, Bill. *Cycles*. England: Pirate Press, 1976.

Helwig, David. *Atlantic Crossings*. San Francisco, Calif.: Ottawa: Oberon Press, 1974.

Hogg, Robert. *The Connexions*. Berkeley, Calif.: Oyez, 1966.

Issa, Kobayashi. *The Year of My Life*. Trans. by Nobuyuki Yuasa. Berkeley, Calif.: University of California Press, 1972.

Kearns, Lionel. *Listen, George*. Calgary: Imago 3, 1965.

Kinnell, Galway. *Book of Nightmares*. Boston: Houghton Mifflin, 1971.

Lee, Dennis. *Civil Elegies*. Toronto: House of Anansi Press Ltd., 1978.

———. 'The Death of Harold Ladoo' in *The Gods* (Toronto: McClelland and Stewart, Ltd., 1979).

Livesay, Dorothy. *The Documentaries*. Toronto: The Ryerson Press, 1968.

McCaffery, Steve. *Carnival, Panel 1*. Toronto: The Coach House Press, 1973.

———. *Carnival, Panel 2*. Toronto: The Coach House Press, 1977.

MacDiarmid, Hugh. 'On a Raised Beach' in *The Hugh MacDiarmid Anthology* (London: Routlege & K. Paul, 1972).

MacFadden, David. *I Don't Know*. Montreal: Véhicule Press, 1979.

———. *The Poet's Progress*. Toronto: The Coach House Press, 1977.

MacKinnon, Barry. *Sex at Thirty One*. Prince George, B.C.: Caledonia Writing Series, 1977.

———. *Songs and Speeches*. Prince George, B.C.: Caledonia Writing Series, 1976.

Marshall, John. *The West Coast Trail Poems*. Lantzville, B.C.: Oolichan Books, 1977.

Miner, Earle, ed. *Japanese Poetic Diaries*. Berkeley, Calif.: University of California Press, 1969.

Neidecker, Lorine. 'My Life by Water' in *Collected Poems* (London: Fulcrum Press, 1968).

Neruda, Pablo. *The Heights of Macchu Picchu*. Trans. by Nathaniel Tarn. N.Y.: Farrar, Straus and Giroux, 1967, c. 1966.

Olson, Charles. *The Maximus Poems*. N.Y.: Jargon/Corinth Books, 1960; Cape Golliard: Grossman, 1968; N.Y.: Grossman, 1975.

Ondaatje, Michael. *The Man With Seven Toes*. Toronto: The Coach House Press, 1969.

———. *The Collected Works of Billy the Kid*. Toronto: House of Anansi Press Ltd., 1970.

Pavese, Cesare. *Hard Labour*. Trans. by William Arrowsmith. N.Y.: Grossman Publishers, 1976.

Perse, Saint-John. *Éloges and Other Poems by Saint-John Perse*. Trans. by Louise Varèse. N.Y.: W.W. Norton, 1944.

Pound, Ezra. *The Cantos*. N.Y.: New Directions, 1948.

Ponge, Francis. *Le Parti pris des choses*. Paris: Gallimard, 1942.

Rimbaud, Arthur. *Illuminations*. Trans. by Louise Varèse. N.Y.: New Directions, 1957.

———. *A Season in Hell*. Trans. by Louise Varèse. Norfolk, Conn.: New Directions, c. 1952.

Reaney, James. *Twelve Letters to a Small Town*. Toronto: The Ryerson Press, 1962.

———. *A Suit of Nettles*. Toronto: Macmillan of Canada, 1958.

Ritsos, Yannis. *Romiossini: The Story of the Greeks*. Trans. by O. Laos. Paradise, Calif.: Dust Books, 1969.

Sinclair, Ian. *Lud Heat*. England: Albion Village Press, 1975.

Sorrentino, Gilbert. *Splendide-Hôtel*. N.Y.: New Directions, 1973.

Spicer, Jack. 'After Lorca', 'The Heads of the Town', and 'Billy the Kid' all in *The Collected Works of Jack Spicer*, Robin Blaser, ed. (L.A.: Black Sparrow, 1975.

Stanley, George. *Mountains and Air*. Terrace, B.C.: Red Queen, 1978.

Stein, Gertrude. 'Tender Buttons' in *Selected Writings* (N.Y.: Random House, 1962).

Thibaudeau, Colleen. *Ten Letters*. Ilderton, Ont.: Nairn, 1979.

Thompson, John. *Stiltjack*. Toronto: House of Anansi Press Ltd., 1978.

Wah, Fred. *Breathin My Name With A Sigh*. Toronto: The Coach House Press, Manuscript Edition, 1979.

———. *Mountain*. Buffalo: Audit/East-West, 1967.

Webb, Phyllis. *Naked Poems*. Vancouver: Periwinkle Press, 1965. Also in *Selected Poems* (Vancouver: Talonbooks, 1971).

William, William Carlos. *Kora in Hell*. San Francisco: City Lights, 1957.

———. *Paterson*. N.Y.: New Directions, 1963.

Zukofsky, Louis. *'A' 1-12*. London: Cape, 1966.

———. *'A' 13-21*. London: Cape, 1969.

———. *'A' 22 & 23*. New York: Grossman, 1975.

———. *'A' - 24*. New York: Grossman, 1972.

Typesetting: Mary Scally & Nelson Adams
Assembly: Sarah Sheard
Presswork: John Ormsby
Edited for the Press by Michael Ondaatje

Typeset in Trump Medieval
and printed in Canada at
The Coach House Press
401 (rear) Huron Street
Toronto, Canada M5S 2G5